Pictures for Language Learning

CAMBRIDGE HANDBOOKS FOR LANGUAGE TEACHERS
General Editors: Michael Swan and Roger Bowers

This is a series of practical guides for teachers of English and other languages. Illustrative examples are usually drawn from the field of English as a foreign or second language, but the ideas and techniques described can equally well be used in the teaching of any language.

In this series:

Drama Techniques in Language Learning – A resource book of communications activities for language teachers
by Alan Maley and Alan Duff

Games for Language Learning
by Andrew Wright, David Betteridge and Michael Buckby

Discussions that Work – Task-centred fluency practice *by Penny Ur*

Once Upon a Time – Using stories in the language classroom
by John Morgan and Mario Rinvolucri

Teaching Listening Comprehension *by Penny Ur*

Keep Talking – Communicative fluency activities for language teaching
by Friederike Klippel

Working with Words – A guide to teaching and learning vocabulary
by Ruth Gairns and Stuart Redman

Learner English – A teacher's guide to interference and other problems
edited by Michael Swan and Bernard Smith

Testing Spoken Language – A handbook of oral testing techniques
by Nic Underhill

Literature in the Language Classroom – A resource book of ideas and activities *by Joanne Collie and Stephen Slater*

Dictation – New methods, new possibilities
by Paul Davis and Mario Rinvolucri

Grammar Practice Activities – A practical guide for teachers *by Penny Ur*

Testing for Language Teachers *by Arthur Hughes*

The Inward Ear – Poetry in the language classroom
by Alan Maley and Alan Duff

Pictures for Language Learning *by Andrew Wright*

Contents

Contents

Pictures for Language Learning

Andrew Wright

with drawings and photographs by the author

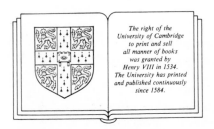

The right of the
University of Cambridge
to print and sell
all manner of books
was granted by
Henry VIII in 1534.
The University has printed
and published continuously
since 1584.

Cambridge University Press
Cambridge
New York   Port Chester
Melbourne   Sydney

Published by the Press Syndicate of the University of Cambridge
The Pitt Building, Trumpington Street, Cambridge CB2 1RP
40 West 20th Street, New York, NY 10011, USA
10 Stamford Road, Oakleigh, Melbourne 3166, Australia

© Cambridge University Press 1989

First published 1989

Printed in Great Britain by Bell & Bain Ltd, Glasgow

British Library cataloguing in publication data
Wright, Andrew
Pictures for language learning. – (Cambridge
handbooks for language teachers)
1. Educational institutions. Curriculum subjects:
England language. Teaching
I. Title
420'.7

Library of Congress cataloguing in publication data
Wright, Andrew, 1937–
Pictures for language learning / Andrew Wright: with drawings by
the author.
    p.   cm. – (Cambridge handbooks for language teachers)
Bibliography: p.
Includes index.
ISBN 0-521-35232-0. – ISBN 0-521-35800-0 (pbk.)
1. Language and languages – Study and teaching – Audio-visual aids.
2. Pictures in education. I. Title. II. Series.
P53.2.W75 1989
418'.007–dc20   89–9976   CIP

ISBN 0 521 35232 0 hard covers
ISBN 0 521 35800 0 paperback

WD

PART D   FINDING, USING AND STORING PICTURES

Contents

Acknowledgements

I would like to thank and acknowledge the following:
– Roger Bowers, Alison Silver, Annemarie Young and Lindsay White for their editorial care, support and guidance.
– Donn Byrne and Brian Heaton for so many ideas for the use of pictures in language teaching.
– Alan Maley and Alan Duff for introducing me to a fresh understanding of the use of pictures in an imaginative way and in particular the use of pictures to promote discussion and expression.
– Mario Rinvolucri, John Morgan, David Hill and other Pilgrim's colleagues for having introduced me to the use of pictures in language teaching as part of personal and social development.
– Irmgard Meyer, Lindsay Miller, Mike Beaumont and students on the Dip.T.E.O. course at Manchester, Ron Adelman and teachers of Thameside for their help in checking through the ideas for their practicality and usefulness.
– All the teachers in so many countries from whom I have learned so much.
– Bill Godfrey for the photograph on p. 129.

The author and publishers are grateful to the following for permission to reproduce copyright material:
Amnesty International, p. 107; Book Club Associates, p. 189; British Rail, p. 107; William Chuckney, p. 88; Bill Godfrey, p. 129; Harvey Barton of Bristol Ltd., p. 86; The Highway Code reproduced by permission of the controller of Her Majesty's Stationery Office, p. 200; The Littlewoods Organisation, pp. 23, 50, 53, 80, 127, 167, 191, 208; London Underground, p. 107; Ordnance Survey, p. 200; Penguin Books Ltd., p. 181; Top Deck Travel, p. 48; VAG (United Kingdom) Ltd., p. 177; Volkswagen UK Ltd., p. 57; Youth Hostels Association, pp. 107, 117.

Introduction

Who is *Pictures for Language Learning* for?

This book is a resource book for teachers who have:
- a specific teaching need, for example, how to introduce a new teaching point or how to find an interesting way of getting the students to argue or express themselves;
- a picture but don't know what to do with it.

It is also for teachers who have:
- any kind of students from beginners to advanced, from children to adults;
- little time for preparation;
- little money or sophisticated media;
- little time and an examination syllabus to follow.

Chief aims of *Pictures for Language Learning*

I would like this book to provide a basis and encouragement for the teacher to invent new ways of using pictures. The many examples of ways of using pictures given in the book have been chosen in order to illustrate the principles described in Part A Pictures in the language classroom.

It was felt to be more useful to have as many examples as possible rather than fewer examples written out more fully. In this way the teacher has a wide range of examples to try out and can see how widely the principles can be applied. It should be noted that the examples given are usually for beginners and intermediate students. However, in virtually every case the examples can be adapted for advanced students or for students studying the foreign language for a special purpose.

None of the ideas in this book require you to buy pictures. Some countries are richer in 'free' pictures than others, but all have some. Part D Finding, using and storing pictures helps the teacher decide what to do with different types of picture and gives some basic suggestions on making and storing pictures.

1   Key considerations

1.1   Why use pictures?

Many language teachers are as concerned to help their students to develop as people and in their ability to relate to others as they are to help them to develop their ability to use the foreign language. For example, it is not enough for students to have a competent ability in a language if they cannot develop a conversation or discussion. In this sense, language teachers have a role as communication teachers and, indeed, as teachers in the broadest sense. It is important to have as wide a range of resources as possible in the classroom so that the students can have a rich base and stimulus for this development. And the resources must include pictures. After all, verbal language is only a part of the way we usually get meaning from contexts. Things we see play an enormous part in affecting us and in giving us information. We predict, deduce and infer, not only from what we hear and read but from what we see around us and from what we remember having seen. Pictures are not just an aspect of method but through their representation of places, objects and people they are an essential part of the overall experiences we must help our students to cope with. This book is intended to help teachers to develop their wider role as teachers of communication.

Specifically, pictures contribute to:
- interest and motivation;
- a sense of the context of the language;
- a specific reference point or stimulus.

1.2   Five basic questions

It is very common to hear people say that pictures are all right for beginners and for young people but not for advanced students or exam classes. This generalisation is unhelpful and untrue. Any activity done in the classroom must be efficient in achieving its purpose. Pictures should certainly be subjected to some practical criteria for assessment of their value, but such criteria should apply to all activities whether they involve pictures or not. The five criteria below provide a way of deciding whether to use an activity or not, whether the activity is a conventional drill or a game making use of pictures.

1 Easy to prepare
Is it easy for you to prepare? If it is difficult for you to prepare in relation to what you will get out of it, then don't do it. If it takes you an hour or two to prepare an activity which you can then use many times with different classes, then it is worth it. Once you have built up a picture library it is usually not difficult to prepare the activities suggested in this book.

2 Easy to organise
Is it easy to organise in the classroom? If it is difficult to organise in the classroom, then don't do it. Opening a textbook is not difficult to organise, but most other activities do require organisational time and energy. The teacher has to decide whether the effort of organising a more complicated activity is worthwhile in terms of the three points which follow.

3 Interesting
Is it interesting to the students? Is it interesting to you? The textbook may be interesting but, on the other hand, you and the students might like to have a change from it. And, of course, the textbook may not be interesting at all! If the activity you are considering is unlikely to interest you and the students, then you will question whether it is worth doing.

4 Meaningful and authentic
Will the language and the way you want the students to use it be authentic and intrinsic to the activity? Would native speakers be at least reasonably happy to use the language in the same way? Students are going to gain more if the language they use is vital to the situation; there should be some reaction or result if they use the language appropriately, or indeed inappropriately. Many conventional language teaching techniques fall down heavily at this point! It is also probably true that many activities which appear to be communicative are little more than empty drills, in the sense that no-one really cares about the meaning.

5 Sufficient amount of language
Will the activity give rise to a sufficient amount of language in order to justify its inclusion in the language lesson? If not, don't do it, unless point 3 above is sufficient justification for you.

3

These five criteria can be applied by any teacher: teachers of advanced adult students or teachers of exam classes, or teachers of beginners. The aim of this book is to offer a store of activities involving pictures which can pass all five criteria and be valid for teachers of all kinds of student.

1.3 Five ways of looking at language

Pictures can be used by teachers and students whatever the emphasis of the syllabus they are following. The examples given in this book cannot cover all possibilities and for that reason it might be of value and interest to show how one picture can be used as a reference and stimulus in order to promote five very different language teaching emphases.

Note The organisation of the activity is not described, only the language which might arise.

1 Structures
The boy is running across the street.   (*present continuous tense*)
She's carrying a stick.   (*subject/verb/object*)
Is it raining?   (*interrogative*)

The picture can be used to illustrate a number of examples of each one of these structures. Although the sentences refer to the picture, there is little importance given to meaning: the emphasis is on structure.

2 Vocabulary
Modern, clean, quiet, suburban, residential. (*different words given for a neighbourhood*)
Old man, young girl, boy, teenager, baby. (*different words given for people*)

3 Functions
Would you mind helping me across the road? (*making a polite request*)
Double-deckers are buses with two floors. (*describing things*)
I like parks in cities. (*expressing likes and dislikes*)

4 Situations
This is a street scene. There is a boy running across the road, who is probably about eight years old. There is also a teenager, who is wondering what to do. There is a bus coming and there is a lot of traffic behind it. If the bus driver stops suddenly there could be an accident, but if he doesn't stop he might run over the boy.
(*describing the situation*)

Teenager: Look out!
Old man: You shouldn't let him play about on the road.
Teenager: I didn't. He just ran into the road.
Old man: It's your fault.
Teenager: I don't know him. I'm a visitor here. I've only just arrived!
(*scripted situation dialogue*)

Squealing of brakes
Teenager:
Bus driver:
Old man:
(*unscripted role play*)

5 Skills
In each of these examples fluency in a skill is developed in a situation which is reasonably authentic.

Listening: The students could be asked to listen to various statements made by witnesses of the incident. They could be asked to pick out any false statements by referring to the evidence in the picture.

Reading: The students could be asked to compare articles about the incident taken from two newspapers and to list differences of emphasis.

Writing: The students could be asked to write a report from the point of view of a witness.

Speaking: The picture could be hidden and the students asked to describe the picture from memory to see how reliable they would be as witnesses.

These brief examples demonstrate that pictures can be used for a variety of purposes: the activities in the body of the book will extend that demonstration. However, the potential of pictures is so great that only a taste of their full potential can be given.

1.4   Activities that matter

Many years ago Professor Pit Corder distinguished between 'talking about' pictures and 'talking with' pictures. This was a helpful distinction because, at that time, the conventional way of using a picture was to describe it. Professor Pit Corder's distinction drew attention to the great variety of potential activities in which pictures can be referred to but not described, for example, looking at a picture of the Eiffel Tower and saying, 'Have you ever been up the Eiffel Tower?' 'Are you frightened of high places?' These more personal responses to pictures are usually more interesting than objective descriptions, for example, 'This is the Eiffel Tower. It is very high.'

Some years later the idea of the need for an 'information gap' was put forward. Once more this was (and is) a most useful concept in general, and in particular when applied to the use of pictures. Basically, the reason for listening and reading is to find out something that we don't know. Sometimes, of course, we read for confirmation of what we know, or we might listen just for the comfort of a friend's concern. However, the concept of 'gap' is an important one in language teaching and provides a ready guide to the validity and usefulness of what we are doing in the classroom. Other gaps have been identified over the years: 'opinion gap' refers to a difference of opinion as a reason for communicating, 'perception gap' refers to people perceiving things differently or perceiving different things and wanting to communicate this.

Without detracting from the usefulness of these distinctions, I would like to argue that there are many gaps which we don't bother to try to cross. We don't choose to talk to everyone about everything just because they might know something we don't know or have an opinion on something we view differently. Many activities in the 'communicative' methods of recent years, whilst based on the idea of a gap, have ignored the idea that in normal life we must want to cross a gap in order to bother to communicate. In other words, there must be a reason which we care about. The ideas for activities in this book are organised and presented with this prime need for a 'reason which matters', based on 'Challenges' and 'Opportunities'.

1.5   Challenges and opportunities

Many of the games and activities suggested for use with pictures in this book are referred to under two broad headings, 'Challenges' and 'Opportunities'. These categories refer to the way in which the learner's mind is engaged and represent a concern with communicative content and personal values.

Challenges

Consider these two activities:

Example 1
Teacher: (*indicating a picture*) Describe this picture for me.
Student A: There's a man.
Student B: There's a tree.
etc.

Example 2
Teacher: (*flashing a picture at great speed*) Did you see anything? Can you tell me what's in the picture? Have another look. (*flashes the picture again*)
Student A: There's a man.
Teacher: Are you sure? Did anyone else see a man?
Student B: It's not a man, it's a woman. She's wearing a red dress and she's got long hair.
etc.

In the first example the students are really being asked, 'Can you remember the foreign words for things in this picture?' But in the second example the students are being challenged to see if they can recognise an image when it is flashed at great speed, and are being asked to use the foreign language in order to communicate what they think. Because students may see aspects of the picture in different ways, they have a reason for speaking and for listening to other students. This simple principle of introducing a challenge can infuse all kinds of activities, making the foreign language a living and vibrant element.

Example 2 above is one of many activities given later in the book under the heading 'Challenge to identify'. Other types of challenge included in the book are challenges to describe, to match, to group, to sequence, to order and to memorise. Other concepts which focus on challenges might include: to predict, analyse, deduce, differentiate, account for, interpret, evaluate, verify and convince. These are familiar words: they are very similar to those used by behaviourists and others in their attempts to define learning outcomes. These attempts were later criticised when learning became increasingly viewed as 'a wandering walk of discovery' rather than the pursuit of specific ends. However, as used in this book such words take on a dynamic rather than a restrictive role: they become moments in the wandering rather than fixed destinations. They can help to stimulate the creativity of the teacher when using a picture.

Opportunities

Very often we do not want to challenge our students, but rather wish to give them an opportunity to do something in a context full of encouragement and free from stress. For example, the teacher might want to encourage the students to talk about themselves, or perhaps to speculate about other people. In such cases, the role of the teacher is to provide a broad suggestion, a gentle stimulus and a helping hand. Consider these two activities.

Example 3

The students look at a number of reproductions of paintings and decide which ones they would like to have, where they would put them and why. For example, 'I would put the Mondrian in my bedroom because it's so calm. It's an abstract picture, so I can imagine anything I like.'

The students could be asked to write a poem to convey how they feel about one of their pictures.

Example 4

The teacher projects a slide of a person. The slide shows the person's appearance and perhaps an indication of where they might be. The students, first of all individually and then in pairs, make notes on who the person might be, their age, interests, occupation, etc. These speculations are then discussed by the whole class. If the teacher has shown a picture of someone he or she knows, the true information can be given and the students' speculations evaluated. The discussion may continue into the more general area of how easy or difficult it is to judge people by their appearance. Students might like to describe how they have misjudged people or indeed how they themselves have been misjudged by others.

In 'Opportunities' the students are encouraged to express feelings and ideas and to exchange experiences, while little or no emphasis is placed on whether these are right or wrong.

In 'Challenges' there is usually a definable goal. The challenge implies an element of competition for the individual or for members of a group. Achieving or not achieving the goal often involves the idea of a right or wrong solution, which is not a feature of 'Opportunities'.

The definable goals of many of the activities categorised under 'Challenges' lead to a predictable need for certain language forms; the language use is thus often 'controlled' or 'partly controlled' by the teacher. In activities categorised under 'Opportunities' the invitation to express ideas and feelings implies less control on the teacher's part of the language needed by the students. Nevertheless, activities in each category include the full range of 'controlled' to 'open' use of language. For example, a student might be 'challenged' to describe a place or a person so that another student can say where or who it is; the description would require a wide range of structures and vocabulary which the teacher could only predict in general terms. On the other hand, students might be 'given the opportunity' to say what they would do if they won a million pounds. The teacher could predict the frequent need to use the second conditional.

'Challenges' and 'Opportunities' are not watertight categories. It is possible, for example, to challenge someone to tell a story even though storytelling usually arises out of a relaxed opportunity to share an experience or an emotion. However, the two categories do provide a useful basis for talking about what we do in the classroom, and for organising pictures so that we can derive the most benefit from them. More importantly, it is hoped that the two categories will provide a stimulus for the teacher to adapt activities and to invent new ones. If the examples given in the book are found useful as they stand, then that is a blessing, but the main purpose of the examples and the way they are organised is to illustrate the principles at work so that the teacher can generate new activities suitable for her or his students. Stimulating challenges and encouraging opportunities, or both together, are at the heart of every lively activity in teaching and learning the spoken and the written language.

1.6 Pictures and class organisation

One of the most useful developments in language teaching methodology in recent years has been in the organisation of students in the
classroom. The gain lies in the degree of interaction between students
and the consequent sense of purpose in using language. Pictures can
play a key role in motivating students, contextualising the language
they are using, giving them a reference and in helping to discipline the
activity.

In this section a few of the many ways of organising classes and
using pictures are described. It is important to note that most of the
activities in the book can be varied by using some of these very different forms of organisation.

There are two basic ingredients to successful organisation: the students should be clear about what they are supposed to do, and they
should have the language to do it.

One useful technique for many of the forms of organisation
described below is to give each student a letter, for example, A or B.
It is then easy to organise the students by saying, 'I want you to work
in pairs; one A and one B together.'

Classwork

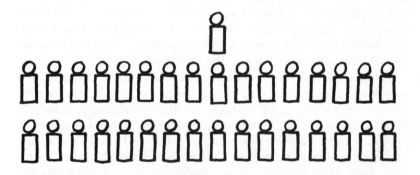

One person, usually but not necessarily the teacher, can, for example,
give instructions or information or (less frequently) be subjected to
questioning.

Example: In the game 'Twenty Questions' one person holds a
picture so that the class cannot see it. The class asks questions to find
out what is in the picture.

Example: In one of the memory games one person stands with his or
her back to a big picture and describes the picture from memory. The
class checks what he or she says.

Circle or U shape arrangement of the whole class for classwork and pairwork. Students can work first with one neighbour, then with the other. The advantage for whole class discussion is that people can see each other properly and that the teacher, if present, is seen more as a member of the group.

Example: The class is shown an ambiguous picture (i.e. a picture which is difficult to interpret). The students discuss with one neighbour their interpretation of the picture. They then turn to their other neighbour to find out what his or her interpretation is.

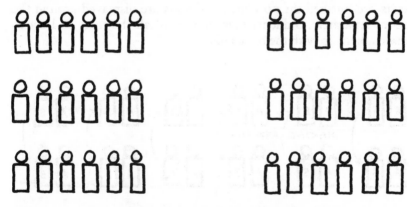

The class is divided into two groups. It is often possible to do this without moving chairs. The organisation can be used for team competitions, drama activities, and mass information-gap activities. It can also be used as a way of demonstrating what is to be done in pairwork.

Example: Show the whole class six pictures to begin with. Then select one of them and only show half the class. Ask them to concentrate on it as hard as they can. Ask the other half of the class if they think they know, telepathically, which picture it is.

11

Pairwork

In the most basic form of pairwork students work with their neighbour, usually without moving from their desks. The students are given some kind of task to carry out: they might play a game, carry out a communication task, work together to solve a problem, or chat about something.

Example: Information-gap games are the most obvious activity for pairwork. For example, in the best known of all information-gap games, one student tries to describe a picture so that the other student can draw it.

Example: Two students can work together on writing the text for a postcard based on a picture postcard they are given. When all the texts are finished the postcards and texts are displayed around the room separately. Students must then read all the texts and try to match them up with the postcards.

In this variation of pairwork, students A and B work together and then new pairs are formed of As and Bs, with the Bs moving. The advantage of this organisation is that each student must take responsibility, but only after working with another student. This inevitably entails the reuse of the same language.

Example: Each pair is given a picture of someone. They decide on a name, occupation, age, family status, likes and dislikes, etc. When B goes to another A he or she must find out by asking questions what the other pair had worked out.

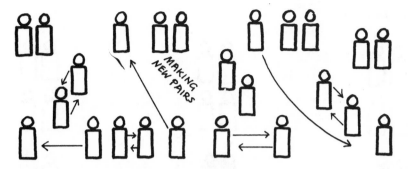

The pairs in this version continually change. For this flexibility it is better to have a space free of desks. If the task is specific and limited it provides an immense amount of practice for every student in a short time.

Example: Each student has either a picture or a textual description of a picture. There is only one text which matches each picture. The students walk around the class working with one student after another until they find their matching text or picture.

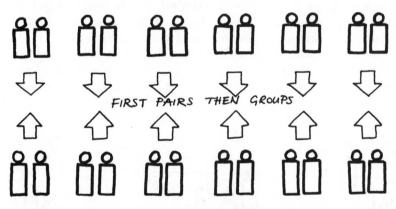

Each pair is given a number of pictures. They attempt to put them into an order and to work out a story (or a description of a process). Each pair then joins another pair, making groups of four. The students in Pair One show their pictures to Pair Two. Pair Two then arranges Pair One's pictures in the order they think Pair One might have chosen and then they try to imagine the story Pair One might have created. The two versions are compared.

The advantages of this organisation are: two students work creatively together listening, speaking and writing. When they compare and tell their stories to the other pair they are supporting each other, though they may not always agree, so they may have to discuss (or argue) with each other.

Groupwork

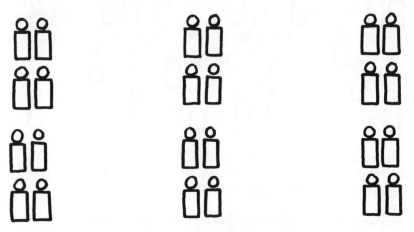

Four to six students are the norm for groupwork. All groups in the class can be given the same work to do or each can work on a different activity. It is an adaptable organisation for cooperative work in which there are enough people for the relationship to be dynamic and yet small enough to encourage even the less able to take part. A great variety of activities can be done in this form of groupwork.

Example: Groups can practise mini-dialogues in which changes within the dialogue are cued by taking a picture from a pile of pictures. This activity is described in some detail in chapter 6 Mini-dialogues.

A has information which the others try to find.

Example: A imagines he or she is hiding in a picture. The others have to find where A is hiding by asking questions.

Groups work together and at the same time interact with other groups.

Example: Each group is given a number to distinguish it from the other groups. Each group is given a picture. All the pictures given out make up a sequence. Individual students from each group go to other groups to find out what each picture shows. They then report back to their group. Each group tries to work out what the order of pictures should be.

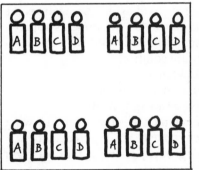 

The students work on a problem together, knowing that each individual student will be responsible for representing the group at the next stage of the organisation.

Note Either completely new groups form or groups divide into pairs and the pairs move to form new groups.

Example: Each student in a group is given a letter, A, B, C or D. Each group is given the same set of pictures representing their country. They are asked to choose only four of them and to rank them in order of importance for giving an impression of the country to people in other countries. The students in each group discuss the selection of pictures and then agree on a choice, if necessary by a vote.

15

New groups are formed. Four As get together, four Bs, etc. Each student then tells the new group what his or her original group decided and argues the case for each picture and for the exclusion of the others.

Note This example, in this form, only works for a mono-cultural group.

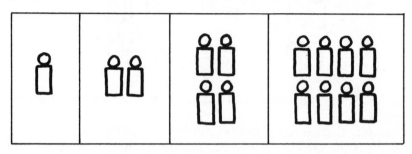

'Pyramid grouping' or 'snowballing'

This is a form of organisation of immense practicality and help in all forms of teaching. It makes each individual take some responsibility, which is an advantage, as sometimes in groupwork some students let the others do the work. The language is used again and again as the case is repeatedly argued. The technique makes the students appreciate that other people can see things differently and that this is of benefit when trying to find an optimum solution.

1. Students begin by working as individuals.
2. Each student then joins another student and they compare their work. They can be asked to arrive at an agreement.
3. Groups of four are now made. Each pair tells the other pair what they have agreed. The group then strive to reach agreement.
4. This is repeated now with two groups, giving a total of eight students.
5. Finally, there is a class discussion of what each group had agreed.

Example: Pyramid grouping is particularly suited to the discussion and evaluation of ideas. However, a very simple way of using the technique is to show a picture and see how many words the students can think of which are related to it. The list of words grows as the students combine their resources. The students can be asked to group the words in some way which is meaningful to them.

Pictures, then, make a particularly powerful contribution to both the content and the process of language learning. In the rest of the book, examples are given of *what* pictures can contribute to the classroom and *how* they can be used.

2   Introduction

Speaking and writing are both productive skills and pictures can often be used in similar ways to promote them. For this reason the two skills are discussed together in this part of the book. The word 'emphasis' is included in the heading because the other skills of listening and reading are also integrated in many of the activities described. Indeed, in some activities described in this part, the receptive skills are equally important. For example, in the well-known activity 'Describe and draw' (see Activity 54), one student gives instructions while the other listens and draws.

2.1   Some roles for pictures in speaking and writing

1. Pictures can motivate the student and make him or her want to pay attention and want to take part.
2. Pictures contribute to the context in which the language is being used. They bring the world into the classroom (a street scene or a particular object, for example, a train).
3. The pictures can be described in an objective way ('This is a train.') or interpreted ('It's probably a local train.') or responded to subjectively ('I like travelling by train.').
4. Pictures can cue responses to questions or cue substitutions through controlled practice.
5. Pictures can stimulate and provide information to be referred to in conversation, discussion and storytelling.

2.2   Controlled and open speaking and writing

Traditionally, teachers have assumed that students learn how to use 'new' language most efficiently if they are allowed to use it in a controlled or guided way first of all. At a later stage the students are given the opportunity to make freer, more open use of the language.

Controlled practice can be very tightly controlled, or loosely guided. Open speaking and writing refers to general conversation, discussion, explanations or personal expression, in which the teacher does not determine the language used by the students.

These ways of referring to language activities may be useful for a book of this kind, but in practice are not so clear cut and are often integrated one with another. For example, when 'new' meanings are presented to the students most teachers will want to get the students to listen and understand, listen and do something, listen and repeat and begin to make use of the new language, all perhaps in the space of a few minutes.

Some teachers might not go beyond the teaching of meaning and controlled practice, giving little opportunity for the creative use of the language. On the other hand, some teachers believe passionately that the 'new' language should be presented and then used by the students in free, natural discussions and conversations immediately.

In most activities suggested in this part of the book, pictures used in controlled practice are as simple and unambiguous as possible. Pictures used to promote general conversation, debate or expression are often more open to a variety of interpretations.

2.3   Mechanical practice and communicative practice

Mechanical practice

In mechanical practice the students concentrate on grammatical or phonological accuracy. Pictures provide motivation and give a non-verbal stimulus for what is said or written. Meaning is given little or no significance. In any case, the teacher usually knows exactly what the student should say.

Teacher: (*showing a picture of a woman jumping*) What's she doing?
Student A: She's jumping.
Teacher: Is she climbing?
Student B: No, she isn't. She's jumping.

Communicative practice

In communicative practice the students make use of the patterns chosen by the teacher but, nevertheless, they and the teacher give value to the meaning of what they are saying. The teacher does not always know exactly what the student wants to say.

Teacher: *(showing the picture of a woman jumping but covering up most of it with another card)* What's she doing?
Student A: She's walking.
Teacher: Is she walking?
Student B: She's running.
Teacher: *(moving down the card so that more can be seen)* Is she running?
Student C: No, she isn't. She's jumping!

2.4   Simulated and real

Simulated activities: This term is used to describe a situation acted out in the classroom which might occur in the future. This is a very necessary way of preparing students for their future use of English. The only danger with it is that it depends largely on long term motivation and the students may not have much of this! If they do not see the reason for the activity it can be a mechanical exercise and not communicative, even though it might appear to give practice in the use of language for relevant purposes.

Real activities: This term refers to the activities which the students want to take part in because the activities seem to be interesting in themselves. The advantage is interest; the disadvantages are that it is not always easy to find interesting activities and also that the students may, if very enthusiastic, want to use their mother tongue.

Real activities can be used as a base for controlled activities. However, by their nature, they tend to lead to a more loosely guided or open use of language.

Examples of simulated and real activities

Simulated: A group of four students. A pile of picture cards of food between them, upside down.
Student A: *(picking up the first picture)* B, do you like ice cream?
Student B: Yes / No / Sometimes.
This activity continues for some time along these lines.

Although Student B answers truthfully, his or her answer doesn't really matter very much. After all, it is not going to get him or her an ice cream! There is a danger that activities like this are thought of as communicative when, very often, the students do not really care what they say if they get the form right. However, these simulated activities do give useful practice. The teacher should only be aware that the students should have as much opportunity as possible to use the language for 'real' purposes.

Real: The class carry out a survey of preferences in food. For example, one student might be given a picture showing a number of different fruits. He or she must ask other students whether they like the fruit 'very much', 'a bit', 'not much' or 'not at all'. When he or she has asked everyone (or an agreed number) the statistics are given to the class.

This is 'real' in the sense that it is a potentially interesting survey to do in the classroom rather than a simulation of a conversation which might happen in the future.

Note 1 It is believed increasingly that the development of the general skill of speaking and writing (fluency) is more important than knowing about individual grammatical rules (accuracy). The majority of the activities in this part of the book contribute to the development of the students' general skill in using the language. The emphasis is on giving the students a reason for speaking and writing. The student consequently thinks more about communicating what he or she wants to say rather than on the form of the language. Nevertheless, many of the activities in this part do give controlled practice in the use of specific language forms. These activities demonstrate that it is possible to combine the experience of using the language with an awareness of the contribution of a particular language form. In this sense such activities provide 'grammar practice'.

Note 2 In order to give as many activities as possible the descriptions are as concise as possible. It is important to appreciate that a student could, in most cases, do what the teacher is described as doing. Most importantly, the majority of activities will be more rewarding if you make use of the group organisational techniques described in section 1.6 Pictures and class organisation.

Note 3 The number and range of examples given in this part of the book illustrate a variety of intentions and styles in speaking and writing: describing people, objects and processes; narrating events; conjecturing; arguing; expressing. As the descriptions of the activities are as concise as possible the 'intentions' and 'styles' are not referred to.

3 Mechanical practice

In mechanical repetition practice the teacher wants the student to concentrate primarily on imitating the sound of the language and is less concerned with meaning. Pictures can be used to motivate the learner and to remind him or her what to say. The teacher might hold up a picture card as a signal for the student to repeat, or point at part of a composite picture. A more demanding activity is when the student tries to remember a number of lines of text and is prompted by a series of pictures (see Activity 2).

In recombination practice and question and answer work the student must adapt the basic sentence pattern. Pictures cue the answers or substitutions (see Activities 4 to 8). Essentially, these activities challenge the student to remember and to manipulate the language forms correctly but there is little or no cognitive or communicative challenge. There is, however, a minor role for such mechanical activities even when the overall aim is for the students to learn to use the language communicatively. Such activities can be seen as the equivalent of finger pull-up exercises for rock climbers.

Repetition

1 Classwork.
Teacher: (*pointing at a picture of two boys who have been fighting*)
Class: (*in chorus and remembering what the teacher has already said*) They have been fighting.

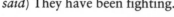

2 **Variation** The teacher points to a series of pictures and the class or individual students repeat the descriptive sentences they have been taught to say. Alternatively, the students act out a dialogue which they have previously been taught, based on the sequence of pictures.

3 **Variation** The teacher points to different parts of a picture or a route through a picture to remind the students what they have to say. The route might be cross-country or through a town. In the example given below, it is the flight of a fly in a room.

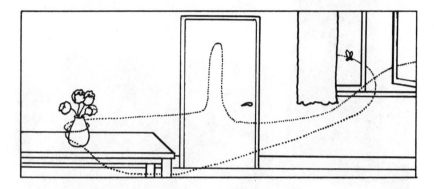

Recombination

Recombination includes: question and answer, substitutions and transformations. Pictures motivate and cue responses non-verbally. The teacher often provides a sentence pattern table to guide the students. Below are a few basic examples of this kind of language practice work:

4 Classwork. The teacher has a pile of picture cards. In this example, the pictures show objects. Alternatives might be: means of transport, places, actions, etc.

Teacher: (*showing a picture of a hat to a student*) What did you do yesterday?

Student: (*using the sentence pattern already given*) Yesterday I bought a hat.

Yesterday I bought a	brush clock hat bag ring T.V.

B

5 **Variation** In order to practise passive forms, the activity above can be followed by showing one of the pictures and indicating that it should be referred to first in the sentence and the agent (the person or thing doing the action) after.

Teacher: (*showing a picture of a hat and then pointing to the student who was referred to as buying it*) The hat was bought by Jenny.

6 **Variation** The teacher shows two pictures of hobbies and actions.

Teacher: (*showing a picture of someone swimming and a picture of someone playing football*) What's John doing?

Student: (*following a given pattern*) He's either (swimming) or (playing) football.

7 **Variation** The students look at a composite picture showing a street scene. The teacher introduces a sentence pattern. The students take the pattern and find different ways of applying it to the picture.

Student: While I was walking down the street I saw (some children playing).

8 **Variation** The traditional use of the composite picture is to ask a variety of questions about it, usually concentrating on a teaching point, for example, the present continuous or prepositions. In the case below it is a future tense.

Teacher: *(pointing to a girl who is obviously just about to find a handbag)* What is the girl going to do?

Student: The girl is going to find the handbag.

Pronunciation

9 Classwork. Pictures can be used to illustrate certain sounds. If the pictures are stuck on cards the word and the sound can be given. Big cards can be used by the teacher for class practice. Small cards can be used by students in games such as 'Pelmanism' (see Activity 171).

3.1   Folding paper and mechanical practice

The nature of paper

Paper can be folded, torn, cut and glued. It can be so thin you can see through it or so thick you can hardly bend it. It can be smooth or rough, mat or shiny. These qualities can be used to create devices which illustrate various language points. Sometimes the device focusses on the language point sufficiently well for it to be used for the presentation of the point. In other cases the language is not so unambiguously illustrated and the device is used more appropriately during practice. In both cases the devices are intriguing to students and contribute to useful and memorable learning.

Using the pictures

The teacher demonstrates the paper devices and gives the example of the language. The students can then handle the device themselves using the language appropriately as the teacher used it. Also, very usefully, the students can make their own paper devices. In the act of inventing and making the devices the students are involved with the language creatively instead of mechanically.

Many of the examples given here have been developed by teachers during in-service workshops.

The face

10   Classwork. Folding strips can be used for teaching or practising vocabulary, as in this device.

The teacher (or the students working in pairs) raises the strips across the face to find the word beneath.

The twins

11 Classwork. In this device the strips are used to contrast facial features.

Teacher: Henry and Bill are twins. Here's Bill. (*pointing to the picture of Bill*) Henry is just like Bill, except (*raising one of the flaps*) Henry has a pointed nose and small ears and Bill has a little round nose and big ears.

Each strip illustrates a contrast between the appearance of Bill and Henry.

A lot of pineapples

12 Classwork. This device contrasts 'a few' and 'a lot of'.

Teacher: (*showing the flap closed*) A few pineapples. (*opening the flap*) A lot of pineapples.

27

The mouse

13 Classwork.

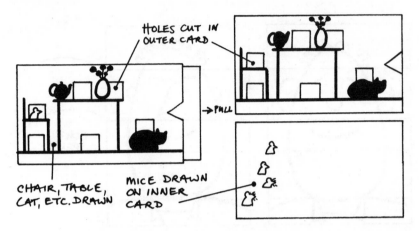

Teacher: (*slowly pulling out the inside card*) The mouse is on the chair. The mouse with whiskers is under the chair. The mouse without whiskers is on the table, between the vase of flowers and the teapot. The mouse with whiskers is under the table. The mouse without whiskers is behind the vase of flowers. Which mouse is going to go behind the cat? The mouse with whiskers!

The bird

14 Classwork.

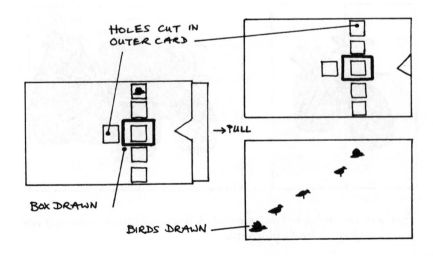

Teacher: (*slowly pulling out the inner card*) The bird is above the box, on the box, next to the box, in the box, under the box and below the box.

Monica in Manchester

15 Classwork. This device illustrates the use of the present simple tense.

Teacher: (*showing the girl's face*) This is Monica.
(*showing the flap*) She lives in Manchester and goes to Parrs Wood School.

The unhappy man

16 Classwork. This device illustrates the use of the word 'except'.

THE TWO SIDES OF
THE CARD SHOWING
THE DRAWING ON
ONE FLAP.

THE THREE STAGES:
IN 1 AND 2 THE FLAP IS
BEHIND. IN 3 THE FLAP IS
IN FRONT.

Teacher: (*showing the picture of the man*) He's an unhappy man except (*turning card around and turning flap over*) when his wife (*turning card around again*) kisses him.

Holly likes swimming

17 Classwork. This device illustrates 'likes' and 'doesn't like'.

Teacher: (*showing the girl's face looking happy*) This is Holly. (*showing the flap*) She likes swimming and playing tennis. (*showing the girl's face looking unhappy*) She doesn't like reading and mathematics.

Judy wakes up

18 Classwork. A number of cards are needed with an action on one side and a clock on the other to illustrate the present tense. It is an advantage to have a special portrait of Judy.

Note It is helpful to have a permanent set of characters.

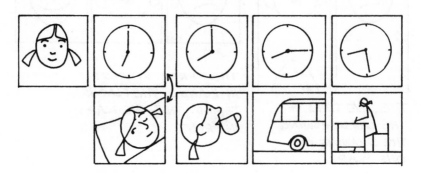

Teacher: (*showing the picture of Judy*) This is Judy. (*showing the first picture of a clock*) What time is it? What does Judy do at that time, do you think? She wakes up. (*When the students have guessed, the card is turned round and the correct guess is confirmed. The teacher props the card on a shelf where everyone can see it, clock side towards the class. Repeating the same procedure with the other cards, the teacher asks what Judy does at each time of the day.*)

The Mobius Strip

19 Individual work. A Mobius Strip is a strip of paper joined at the ends and with a twist. Instead of making a Mobius Strip the teacher can make a 'belt'. As the strip is moved round and round between the fingers one has the feeling of something being repeated, and that is the nature of this use of the present simple.

Any sentence can be written which seems to go on and on. The sentence written here is: 'In the morning I wake up and then eat and then work, sometimes I see my friends or go for a run, and then I work again until about midnight and then . . . (the sentence is now repeated from the beginning).

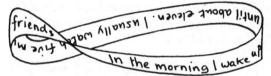

TWIST THE ENDS OF THE STRIP AND STICK THEM BEFORE YOU WRITE YOUR SENTENCE!

Every day and Sundays

20 Classwork. Sometimes it is helpful to work on two language points at the same time, particularly if they are often confused. The present continuous and present simple tenses are illustrated with this device.

TODAY!

Teacher: (*showing the device with the flap closed*) Usually she works in an office, but (*folding back the flap*) today she's dancing.

She's going to dive

21 Classwork. The knowledge that the flap will open implies that something is going to happen and this contextualises the future with 'going to'.

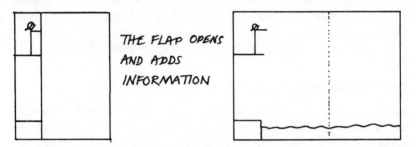

Teacher: (*showing the picture*) What is she going to do? (*then opening out the flap and confirming whether the students were right or not*)

Fortune-teller

22 Classwork. The fortune-teller contextualises the future tense with 'will'. 'Will' may be used for a future which is beyond our control and in this sense the prediction of future events with a fortune-teller clearly conveys the special quality of 'will'.

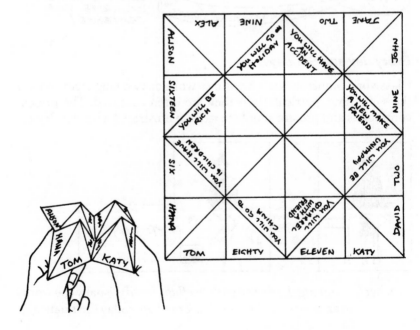

32

Fortune-tellers like the one shown above are well known in most countries of the world. There is usually a student in the class who can remember how they are made. Older students can easily be persuaded to make these fortune-tellers by saying that they will be used with another class or to entertain children. After seeing the teacher's fortune-teller students must make their own and write their own predictions.

Teacher: (*Holding the fortune-teller as shown and asking a student to choose a name on the outside of the fortune teller.*
Spelling out the name and moving the fortune-teller in and out.
Showing the student the numbers inside and asking him or her to choose one.
Counting up to the number chosen, moving the device in and out.
Showing the student the numbers again and asking him or her to choose a number. Then opening out the paper and reading out his or her fortune, i.e. what will happen to him or her.)

23 Variation The design below is a less complicated version of the fortune-teller. The illustration shows the two sides of the card.

Teacher: (*Introducing the fortune-teller and asking the students to call out any number on the card.*
Lifting up a flap when a student calls out a number and reading out his or her fortune.)

Eating too much

24 Classwork. This device illustrates 'If' and the future with 'will'.

THE FLAP CHANGES

THE INFORMATION

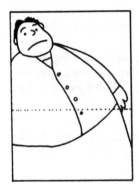 

Teacher: (*showing the picture with the flap up*) If you eat too much ... (*showing the picture with the flat down*) you will get fat. (*showing the picture with the flap up*) If you eat too many sweets ... (*showing the picture with the flap down*) you will get toothache.

A story strip

25 Classwork. This device illustrates the present continuous, future with 'going to', and the past simple.

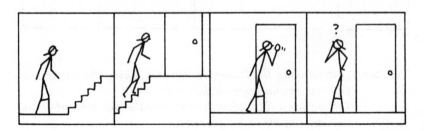

ALL THE PICTURES ARE
FOLDED BACK AND
BEHIND

The first illustration above shows the complete story (although it could be made to continue around the reverse side).

Teacher: (*having folded the device and showing the first picture only*) What is she doing? What is she going to do?
(*Still showing the first picture and asking the class to guess what she is going to do next.*
Asking what she is going to do in each of the successive pictures.
Asking the students to retell the whole story.) She climbed the steps.

She's going to sit on the cat

26 Classwork. The three flaps illustrate the future with 'going to', the present continuous, and the present perfect.

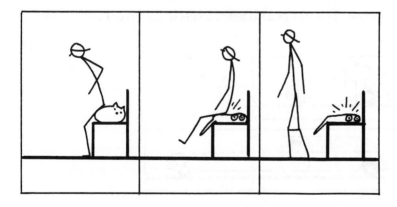

Teacher: (*showing the first picture*) She's going to sit on the cat.
(*either showing the first two pictures together or showing the second by itself*) She's sitting on the cat. (*either showing all three pictures together or the last one by itself*) She's sat on the cat.

The monk

27 Classwork. The two flaps in this device reveal how the monk used to behave.

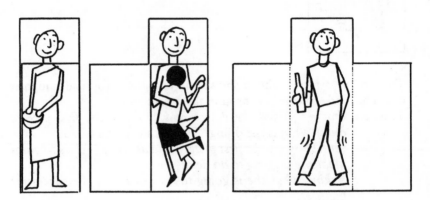

Teacher: (*showing the picture of the monk*) He's a monk. (*opening the first flap and showing what he used to do*) He used to dance. (*opening the second flap and showing what else he used to do*) And he used to drink.

He's got a big car

28 Classwork. This device also helps to illustrate 'used to'.

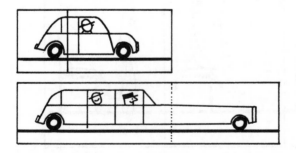

THE FLAP OPENS!

Teacher: (*showing the little car*) He used to have a little car. (*opening the flap and showing the big car*) But now he's got a big one.

He used to be fat

29 Classwork.

Teacher: (*showing the thin man*) He's thin now. (*opening the flap and showing the fat man*) But he used to be fat.

Three tenses

30 Classwork. This device illustrates the present continuous, present perfect continuous and past simple.

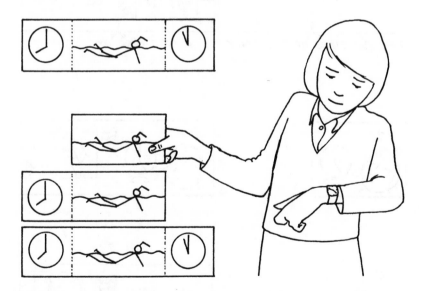

The first drawing shows the complete piece of paper. The second drawing shows what the students see to begin with.

Teacher: (*showing the picture of the man swimming*) What's he doing? He's swimming. (*turning the flap and showing the clock furthest from the teacher and the action, and then looking at his or her watch, representing the present moment*) He's been swimming for two hours and twenty minutes (for example). (*opening both flaps and showing both clocks, which represent the starting and finishing of the action*) He swam from eight o'clock until eleven o'clock.

The alarm clock

31 Classwork. This device illustrates the past simple and 'If' plus the past perfect.

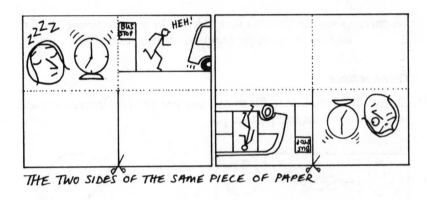

THE TWO SIDES OF THE SAME PIECE OF PAPER

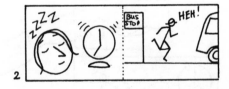

RAISING THE FLAPS AND
CHANGING THE PICTURES

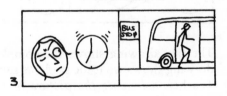

The first two illustrations show the two sides of the same piece of paper.

Teacher: (*showing the first picture*) It was seven o'clock. The alarm clock rang but she didn't wake up. (*showing the second picture together with the first*) So she missed her bus. (*raising the flap and changing the first picture*) If she had woken up … (*raising the flap and changing the second picture*) she wouldn't have missed her bus.

The ghost

32 Classwork. The use of the past continuous and the past simple is shown when a continuing action in the past is suddenly interrupted.

The complete card is shown in the first illustration.

Teacher: (*showing the first scene and describing it*) It was midnight. The cat was sleeping in front of the fire, the woman was playing the piano, the man was singing, and the moon was shining. Suddenly there was a knock on the door.
(*knocking on a table then opening the door in the device*)
(*changing the picture and saying what happened*) It was a ghost! The cat jumped up, the woman fell off her stool, and the man shouted, 'Help!'

Smoking is bad for you

33 Classwork. The story strip illustrates the present simple, the present perfect continuous and 'used to'.

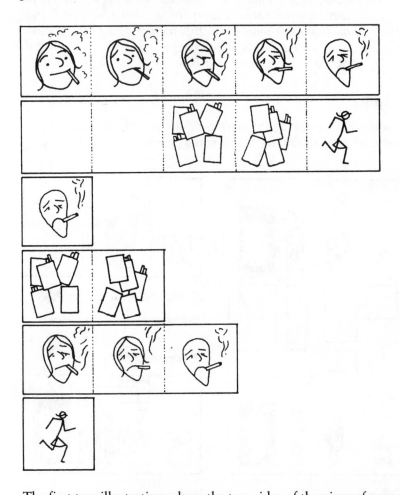

The first two illustrations show the two sides of the piece of paper.

Teacher: (*showing the picture of the old woman*) She smokes cigarettes. (*showing the packets of cigarettes on the other side of the paper*) She smokes ten packets of cigarettes every day. Two hundred cigarettes!
(*returning to the woman and slowly unfolding all the pictures showing how many years she has been smoking*) She's been smoking for years: one, two, three, four, five years!
(*closing up the concertina of paper, then turning it round to show the young woman*) She used to go jogging!

40

4 Communication and challenges

4.1 Challenge to describe

In most of the activities which follow, the student is challenged to describe something so well that another student can identify it by pointing, drawing, commenting, etc.

Say anything you know

34 Classwork. The class is shown a picture of a scene (or a lot of individual pictures). The students say anything they can about it. This is an opportunity for the least able to call out any word they know which could name part of the picture or be related to it in some way; the more able can offer fuller sentences which might be objective descriptions, interpretations or personal associations. It is a communicative use of language in the sense that the teacher cannot be sure what they will say, but it is not random in the sense that the words must relate to the picture. It is satisfying for the students to see their suggestions written on the board.

35 **Variation** The students work in pairs, writing down every word they can think of related to the picture.

36 **Variation** The class is shown a complicated picture. Each student writes down as many words as he or she can which describe things in the picture. Students then join their neighbours and compile a joint list. Groups are formed and compile a final list.

Competition can be introduced between groups of students for the greatest number of words. The teacher might find it profitable to discuss how to group the words. Extra 'points' might be given for 'special' words.

Examples of semantic groupings: animals, things with straight sides, things which have metal in them. Examples of language groupings: nouns, verbs, words with similar stress patterns.

37 **Variation** With the above activity and most of the others in this section the students can be asked to write descriptive sentences which

deliberately include gaps which are then filled in by other students. The gaps can be random or might be restricted to verbs, nouns, articles, prepositions, etc.

Note 1 Any pictures can be used for this activity. Small pictures of scenes can be used in groupwork rather than a big wall picture for the class as a whole.

Note 2 Even near beginners may know too many words for this activity. In this case, the teacher can say what aspect of the picture is to be described, for example, what people are doing, where things are, what things are made out of, how people feel.

Describe a picture

38 Individual work. Each student is given a picture by the teacher. He or she writes a description of the picture. The teacher collects all the pictures and displays them. The descriptions are collected and then redistributed to the students so that each student gets another student's description. Each student must then find the picture to match his or her description.

39 **Variation** About twenty pictures are displayed. The students walk about and look at them all. Each student then writes a text based on one of the pictures. The descriptions are then displayed (or read out) and all the students try to match each description to a picture.

40 **Variation** Each student writes a letter describing a person to be met at an airport or station based on one of twenty pictures of people on display. The description in the letter must then be matched with the pictures.

41 **Variation** Each student writes a description of a lost object which must then be matched against the displayed pictures. If a lot of the pictures are of similar objects, the challenge would be more difficult.

42 **Variation** The picture might be a cartoon or a photograph from a newspaper and the text a caption.

Crosswords

43 Pairwork. Students design a crossword and write the clues for it related to a complicated picture, i.e. all the answers are to be found in the picture. Crosswords can be relatively simple to design.

Guess what and where

44 Classwork or groupwork. The class looks at a complicated picture. One student describes part of the picture and the other students say what is being described.

45 **Variation** Groupwork. The students study a number of different pictures, for example, postcards. One student describes one of the pictures and the others say which one it is.

Who is thinking that?

46 Classwork or groupwork. The class is shown a complicated picture or a number of pictures. Each student describes the thoughts of someone in the picture. The other students say who is thinking those thoughts.

Who is saying that?

47 Pairwork. The class is shown a complicated picture or a number of pictures. A pair of students imagine a conversation which two people, among many others in a picture, might be having. The students act out their dialogue for another pair who try to identify which people in the picture are being referred to.

Note 1 This activity gives an opportunity for discussing levels of formality and informality.

Note 2 Cartoon drawings are useful for this activity.

Part B Emphasis on speaking and writing

Where am I?

48 Classwork. A complicated picture is shown to the class. The teacher says he or she is a mouse and hiding in the picture. The students must guess where he or she is hiding.
Student: Are you behind the tree?
Student: Are you in the old man's pocket?

Happy holidays

49 Individual work. Each student is given a postcard of a holiday place. The student writes a text on a separate piece of paper. All the cards are displayed and all the texts are collected and redistributed so each student gets a text written by another student. Each student must find out where his or her friend was staying, i.e. which postcard they were referring to.

Note It is more amusing if the students are inventive.

Who am I?

50 Classwork. A complicated picture is shown to the class. The teacher imagines that he or she is a particular person or object in the picture. The students must ask questions to find out who (or what) the teacher is.

51 **Variation** The teacher thinks of two different people from amongst about ten people in a picture. The students ask questions to find out which two the teacher is thinking of. The form of the questions and answers can give practice in certain language forms, for example:
Student A: Is either of them wearing a hat?
Teacher: One of them is.
Student B: Has either of them got bags?
Teacher: No, neither of them has.

What happened to me?

52 Classwork. The teacher draws several pictures and maps on the board which illustrate an experience in his or her life. The students ask questions to find out what happened. This activity naturally makes use of past tense forms.

Letters of complaint

53 Individual work. Each student is given a picture of an object or a place (hotel, holiday site, restaurant). The student must then write a letter of complaint about the object or place. It is easier for the students if they are encouraged to exaggerate and to use their imagination, indeed to make the complaint as ridiculous as possible.

Describe and draw

54 Pairwork. One student has a picture or a plan, but does not show it to his or her partner. He or she tries to describe it so that the other student can make an accurate drawing of it. The 'artist' can ask questions and both must work together to make the drawing as accurate as possible.

55 **Variation** The 'artist' is given a drawing, plan or diagram which he or she must complete, for example, by drawing hair onto a person or colouring in the clothes. The second drawing with things missing in it can be made by photocopying a drawing and whitening out parts.

56 **Variation** The picture or plan is described from memory instead of from an actual picture. For example, a student might describe his or her bedroom.

57 **Variation** A student is asked to draw a picture on the board instructed by the whole class who can see a picture the 'artist' cannot see.

58 **Variation** Each student writes a letter describing his or her bedroom (favourite room, garden, district, fantasy island). Students exchange letters and then try to draw what the letter describes.

Note 1 The teacher should be confident that the students have appropriate language to describe the picture.

Note 2 The teacher might like to concentrate on situations in which spatial relations are important, for example, maps and buildings or room plans and furniture.

Note 3 Most of the variations above could be done with a written description.

Note 4 In the pairwork and classwork activities above 'the artist' can be blindfolded.

Describe and arrange

59 Pairwork. Student A has an arrangement of pictures and Student B has the same pictures but cut up and loose. Student A must tell Student B how to arrange his or her pictures. Sometimes a magazine page has a lot of pictures together, so a photocopy can be made of it and then the page cut up. Alternatively, a lot of small pictures can be arranged on a photocopying machine and photocopied.

Note All the pictures can be chosen to give practice in specific language points, for example, words for feelings with pictures of facial expressions; prepositions with pictures showing the same objects in different positions; pronunciation with pictures requiring concentration on fine differences of sound to differentiate between them.

Happy twins

60 Classwork. If there are 30 students in the class, fifteen pairs of pictures must be provided. (This can be done by photocopying.) Each student is given a picture. The students walk about the class describing their picture and asking other students about theirs until they find a student with a matching picture.

Note Pairs can be: (1) identical; (2) two halves of the same picture which has been cut up; (3) pictures representing opposites; (4) pictures representing 'before' and 'after'; (5) a famous person and what he or she is famous for, etc.

61 **Variation** For a class of 30 students, fifteen pictures must be provided. Each pair of students is given one picture, and they must then write a short description of the picture. The teacher collects all the pictures and the texts (having made sure that the descriptions are reasonable, though not necessarily grammatically correct). The teacher then redistributes the pictures and the descriptions randomly round the

class so each student either gets a picture or a written description. Students must then find which other student has the picture to match their text or the text to match their picture.

62 **Variation** Pairwork. Each pair working together will need about sixteen pictures, many of which are identical pairs. It is important that the pictures are the same shape and size. The pictures are mixed and placed in a pile upside down. Each student takes it in turns to pick one up without showing it to the other. Then each student describes his or her picture. They can ask each other questions. If they decide they have a pair, they place them on the table. If the pictures are a pair they put them on one side; if they are not an identical pair they replace them in the pile.

Lost property

63 Groupwork. Each student (except one) is given three pictures of luggage or objects which are useful when travelling. They study them and then give them all to the other student who then pretends to be a clerk in a lost property office. The students take it in turns to describe the objects they have lost in order to get them back. If some of the objects are similar the activity is more interesting, for example, one bag might be red, another blue, and another blue and red.

64 **Variation** Each picture is stuck on a card together with a place and a time of day. The clerk can then ask where and when the object was

lost. Once more, if some of the times and places are identical then the students must be precise, and the students who are not speaking must listen carefully or another student will get their property!

65 **Variation** The group is made of two pairs of students and is given twenty small pictures of objects. Each picture has a different number on it. Five pictures are given to each student, who does not show them to anyone, not even his or her partner. (Indeed, it is better to decide who the partners will be after this stage in the activity.) Each student writes down a description and the number of each of his or her five objects. The twenty pictures are then collected, shuffled and placed face down in a pile. Then each student takes it in turns to pick up a picture and to describe it to his or her partner. The description must not include the name of the object nor the number of the picture. If the partner thinks it is his or her 'lost property' the partner claims it and can keep it if the number is one of the five he or she wrote down at the beginning of the activity.

Ambiguous pictures

66 Classwork and groupwork. The teacher draws an ambiguous picture on the board.

The students say what they think the picture is illustrating. The teacher encourages differences of opinion and is careful not to support any particular interpretation. Argument can be encouraged about the interpretations. The teacher can then add more information to the drawing, making it less ambiguous.

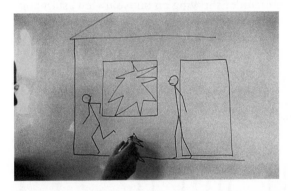

Personal experiences related to the subject of the picture can then be described and discussed, for example, 'Have you ever broken a window? What happened?' There may be an opportunity to raise more general issues, resulting from the conversation about personal experiences, for example, 'Should she or he have been punished? What is the role of punishment in society?'

Dialogues can be written relating to the interpretation, for example, about what the people might be saying in the picture.

Note Dialogues can be imagined which are not only taking place during the time of the picture, but before or after.

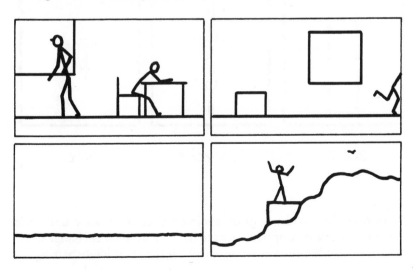

4.2 Challenge to identify

In this type of activity the student is challenged to identify and name a picture or part of a picture which is difficult to recognise. There are several ways of making common objects and actions difficult to recognise. These ways include: showing an unusual view, showing a detail, showing the picture at speed, showing the picture out of focus.

Unusual views

67 Classwork or groundwork. The teacher shows an unusual view of an object or a detail and asks the students to try to identify it.
Teacher: What's this? / What are these?
Student: It's a table.

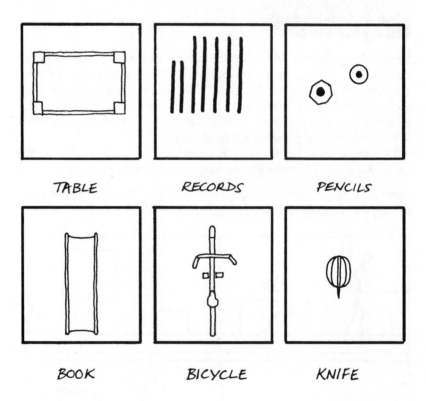

TABLE   RECORDS   PENCILS

BOOK   BICYCLE   KNIFE

68 **Variation** The students draw their own unusual view and write several possible descriptions next to it. Students then exchange drawings and descriptions and decide which is the most likely pairing.

This is a jet engine.
It is a modern picture.
It is an electric cooker.
These are windows in a ship.

Picture details

69 Classwork or groupwork. The teacher shows part of a picture and asks the students to identify it. The teacher can do this by covering over a big picture so that only a small part of it can be seen, or by cutting a small piece of a picture out of a large picture. Alternatively, flaps can be hinged over a picture: the students have to guess what is beneath.

When using a slide projector, a piece of paper with a hole in it or a cardboard roll can be placed over the end of the lens. The hole in the paper or the roll selects a small circle of detail on the projected image. If the roll is moved the revealed detail changes. Students can be asked what they think each detail is and asked what they think the picture as a whole will look like. The picture can then be shown without the roll.

Note If details of the face of a famous person are shown the language will be, 'Who is this?' 'Whose mouth is this?' etc.

70 **Variation** The students can cut small pieces from a large picture and then write a number of descriptions next to each small piece, only one of which is true. Students then exchange pictures and descriptions and decide which is the true description.

He's riding a horse.
He's playing golf.
He's riding a motorbike.
He's playing cricket.

He's wearing trainers.
He's wearing sandals.
He's wearing cycling shoes.

71 **Variation** Flaps of paper can be hinged over a picture so that the teacher can show small bits of the picture only. The students try to identify what the detail is and they then try to guess what the whole picture might look like.

72 **Variation** Groupwork. A jigsaw is made by cutting a picture into square pieces. Each student is given one piece. The group is also given a piece of paper the same size as the jigsaw, with squares on it. Each student then takes it in turns to describe their piece of the picture, without showing the others. The rest of the group listens and tries to decide where that piece of the jigsaw fits. Only when the position of all the pieces has been guessed at are they laid down to check the accuracy of the guesses.

Flashing a picture

73 Classwork. The teacher flashes a picture repeatedly at the class, asking the students to say what they saw each time. The teacher encourages differences of opinion and does not confirm any of the ideas. The students are more involved if they are asked to discuss what they see with their neighbour.

The picture can be a picture card or can be flashed on an overhead projector by placing a piece of card above the picture or objects, or on a slide projector by covering the end of the lens with a book. If the picture is very simple then the teacher can predict the language which will be needed (controlled). If the picture is more complicated then the students will want to use all the language at their command (open).

Slide out of focus

74 Classwork. The teacher shows a slide totally out of focus. The students try to imagine what the picture might be. They can be asked to write down their ideas and to compare them with their neighbour before offering their opinions to the class as a whole. The teacher brings the slide into focus very slowly, stopping perhaps four times to ask the students to revise their opinions.

C

Invisible drawing

75 Classwork or groupwork. The teacher draws something in the air with a finger, for example, an elephant. The class tries to identify what the teacher has drawn.

76 **Variation** Pairwork or groupwork. A student draws with a finger on a desk or table top.

4.3 Challenge to match

In most of the activities below, the students are challenged to find a relationship between two bits of information. The relationship might be objective, for example, between a description and a picture, or subjective, for example, between a poem and a picture. The information might be verbal or pictorial or both.

Gift game

77 Classwork. The students have a number of pictures of objects and decide which object they would give as a present to different relatives or friends.

78 **Variation** A pile of pictures of objects is placed face down on a table. Each student is given three pictures of people. (These pictures of people can be 'amusing' or 'serious', and the students can refer to them as relatives, friends or acquaintances.) The students take it in turns to pick up a picture and to say why they would give it to one of their people as a present. If the other students think it is a good reason, the first student can keep the picture. The aim is to collect as many presents as possible for each person.

56

Student: (*picking up a picture of a hen*) This is for my friend. She likes fresh eggs.

Imaginative matching

79 Classwork or groupwork. Two pictures are chosen at random and the students are challenged to find a connection between them. The teacher can hold up two picture cards in order to challenge the class as a whole. In groupwork, there can be a pile of pictures upside down. The students take it in turns to take two, place them picture side up and then, using their imaginations, say why they are connected.

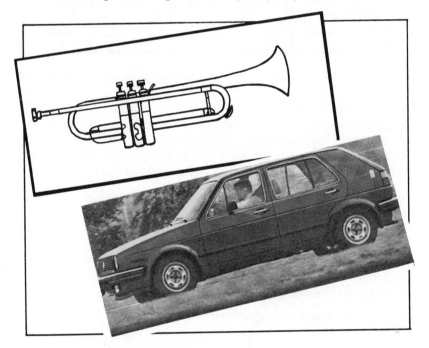

Student A: They are both made out of metal.
Student B: The man was playing the trumpet while he was driving.

80 **Variation** Using picture cards and word cards the students take it in turns to make a sentence using the word and referring to the picture.

Find the difference

81 Pairwork. Each student has a picture which the other student cannot see. The students must find out, through discussion, the similarities and the differences between their pictures. For example, in each of the

pictures below there is a house with a door and three windows. However, in one picture there is a door in the middle and three windows, and the other picture has these too, but there are also two trees, a lot of dark clouds and high mountains.

Note 1 Differences can be designed to give practice in specific language forms, for example, comparatives, numbers or prepositions. (For example, 'The man's nose is longer in picture 1 than in picture 2'; 'There are 21 spoons in picture 1 and 23 in picture 2'; 'The mouse is under the table in picture 1 but it's in the cupboard in picture 2'.

Note 2 There are two easy ways of producing drawings with minor differences.
1. Draw a picture and then lay another piece of paper over it. Trace the drawing, making minor changes in the copy.
2. Photocopy a drawing. Use typist's correction fluid to remove details, and change details with a fine black pen. Photocopy the adapted drawing.

Note 3 Two magazine pictures of similar objects or scenes can also be used.

82 **Variation** Classwork. The teacher shows each picture, separately, for a few seconds. The students then discuss the differences. The teacher shows the pictures again together, and once again the students discuss the differences they noticed and remembered.

Picture theatre

83 Groupwork. Each group is given a reproduction of a painting showing various people in a scene. The groups study their picture and then give it back to the teacher. The teacher displays all the pictures together. The groups then arrange themselves in the same positions as

the people in their picture. Other groups must decide which picture they are representing.

Note The language practice arises out of the discussion about who will represent the various people in the picture and where they are to place themselves. Classroom furniture can be used to represent objects in the picture. It is advisable to have one or two students as 'producers' of the scene.

True or false

84 Classwork. The activities described below are examples of a very big family of games in language teaching called 'True/False'. One student, or the teacher, says something about a picture which is either true or untrue. The other students must correct him or her if the statement is untrue.

In a very simple version of this game the teacher holds up a picture card:

Teacher: (*showing a picture of a woman playing tennis*) She's playing squash.

Students: No, she isn't. She's playing tennis.

85 **Variation** This true/false game can be used at the repetition stage of a lesson when the teacher wants the students simply to repeat what he or she says. The teacher can hold up a picture and make a statement which is true or false. If the statement is true, the students repeat what the teacher says. If it is false, they remain silent. In this way the students have the advantage of repetition practice with its emphasis on pronunciation, but at the same time must think about the meaning of what they are saying. The teacher can add humour to the activity by pretending to be tired or shortsighted. This 'explains' why the teacher is making so many mistakes.

86 **Variation** Instead of using a single picture card the teacher can describe parts of a wall picture.

87 **Variation** The students are given a lot of sentences about a picture, some of which are true and some of which are false. They copy out all those which apply to a picture they are shown.

88 **Variation** The students are given a text describing a picture, which contains false statements. The students rewrite the text accurately.

89 **Variation** The students are given different texts describing a picture correctly. They rewrite their text introducing untrue elements. The students then exchange texts and try to find the untrue elements in each other's work.

90 **Variation** Students working in pairs write true and/or false sentences describing a picture. The pairs of students exchange sentences and decide which sentences written by the other pair are true and which are false.

91 **Variation** The students draw a number of optical illusions and then write descriptive sentences next to the illusions, which may be true or false. They then exchange their work with another student and each student examines the illusion and decides whether the statements are true or false.

Note The student originating the illusion uses a ruler or protractor, etc. The student receiving the work must try to judge it by eye.

Line C is the longest line.

Line B is longer than line A.

Line D is longer than line E.

Angle G is wider than angle F.

4.4 Challenge to group

Challenge to group is an extension of Challenge to match. In these activities the students must find a relationship between more than two bits of information. This relationship might be objective, for example, if the students are asked to group foods under headings such as meat, fruit, etc., or subjective, for example, if they are asked to group a number of pictures according to feelings: gentleness, violence, etc.

Grouping pictures

92 Classwork and/or groupwork. The students are given a number of pictures (for example, twenty postcards) and are asked to arrange them into groups. Students can do this individually to begin with, and make notes. Then they can work with other students and, through discussion, agree on a variety of ways of categorising the postcards. The postcards might be grouped, for example, under: seaside, country and town, sport; shopping; climate; whether the students would like to go there, etc. It is usually possible to find many ways of grouping pictures.

93 **Variation** The groups divide up so that two students stay with the pictures and two join another group; then the discussion can continue with the new students trying to find out why the groupings have been decided upon.

Picture jigsaws

94 Classwork. A number of pictures are required, each of which should be glued onto card and then cut into pieces. There should be the same number of pieces as there are students in the class. For example, for a class of 30 there could be five pictures, each cut into six pieces. The pictures can be as small as postcards, and the pictures themselves should be quite different, for example, a landscape, a cityscape, a crowd of people, some animals. The students should be able to name what they see in their bit of their picture, for example, 'It's a man's leg.' 'He's wearing grey trousers.' (See Challenge to identify.)

Each student is given a part of a picture. The students must then walk around the room and describe their bit of picture and ask other students, one by one, to describe theirs, without showing their piece of picture. When they think they have found a student with a piece from the same picture they stay with that student and look for other students with bits from the same picture. Finally, they put all the pieces from one picture on a table together and reconstitute it.

95 **Variation** Pairwork. The above activity can be done with pairs of students first studying the piece of picture and then walking around together. Furthermore, having studied the piece of picture they can be asked to give it to the teacher and then must concentrate on describing it from memory.

96 **Variation** Groupwork. A picture is cut into small squares and each student given one or two of these squares. The group is also given a piece of paper with squares drawn on it of the same size as the jigsaw squares. Each of the squares is numbered. Each student then takes it in turns to describe his or her piece(s) of the picture. The group then try to work out where each piece of the picture fits on the squared paper (still without the whole group seeing all the pictures). When the group has guessed the position of the pictures each student lays his or her piece(s) on the squares where the group thought they would fit, and at this point they can see if they had guessed correctly!

Connections

In the many variations for this activity the students must say what connection they find between the pictures they have. The different variations of this activity could be categorised under Challenge to describe, Challenge to match or Challenge to group. They are all listed here as they are so closely related.

97 Groupwork. Each student is given six pictures. The students take it in turns to lay down two pictures. They must think of a connection between the two pictures and tell the other students. If the other students think that what has been said is acceptable then the pictures can be left on the table. The word 'acceptable' must be interpreted according to the level and interests of the students as well as the picture connections they are making. For example, a beginner might put down a picture of a car and a picture of a boy and say, 'He likes cars.' This would be acceptable. Intermediate learners might say that such a sentence is too boring and insist on something else. An acceptable sentence at intermediate level might be, 'He wants to get his driving licence as soon as possible.' The aim is for each student to lay down all his or her picture cards.

98 **Variation** As above, but each student lays down one picture and argues that there is a connection between his or her picture and one already on the table.

99 **Variation** This variation is based on the game of 'Snap'. Small picture cards and small word cards are required. The word cards name or describe each of the picture cards or are linked with each picture (for example, a sentence which might be spoken by a person in the picture). There should be enough cards for each student to have six of each.

Each student is given, at random, six pictures and six word cards which are not necessarily pairs. If the first player has, by chance, two cards which make a pair, he or she can lay them both down on the table. If the other students agree that they are a pair they can be turned over. Then the first student must lay down a picture or a word card by itself. The moment he or she lays the card down any other student can shout 'Snap' and put down the card which pairs with it. If the pairing is correct then the two cards are placed upside down.

The aim is for each student to get rid of all his or her cards. The game is more exciting if there are several identical pairs so that two students must then compete to get their card down first.

100 **Variation** A minimum of nine pictures are laid down in a simple grid pattern. Students work either by themselves or in pairs. If they can argue for a connection between a row of three or more pictures they can remove them. The aim is to be able to remove them all.

Note The students can be asked to write down a sentence which connects the pictures. In this way the teacher can check on what happened.

THE APPLE, BOOK, CUP LINE COULD BE REMOVED.

While he was reading he ate an apple and drank a cup of tea.

Happy families

01 Groupwork. Pictures mounted on card and in sets of four are required, for example, vegetables, fruit, household objects, sports, transport. The other pictures belonging to the set are written on each card, for example, vegetables: potato, cabbage, carrot, onion. (Other ways of defining sets could be used, such as word sounds, grammatical points, etc.) There should be enough for each student in a group to have eight pictures.

Eight pictures are given at random (i.e. from different sets) to each student. The student must decide which picture families to collect. For example, if the student has two or more vegetable pictures he or she may decide to collect vegetables. The students take it in turns to ask other students if they have a card in the set they are looking for.

Student A: Have you got a cabbage?
Student B: Yes, I have.
Student A: May I have it, please?
Student B: Yes, here it is.

If a student has a picture which is asked for he or she must hand it over.

102 **Variation** Pictures about 10 cm × 20 cm are pasted onto card and then cut up into parts which can be named, for example, 'cat's leg', 'cat's tail'. If there are four players there should be four complete pictures. The various parts of the four pictures should be mixed up and then shared out between the players. Each player must decide which picture to collect (guided by how many pieces he or she has of the picture to begin with).

Student A: Have you got a cat's leg?
Student B: Yes, I have.
Student A: May I have it, please?
Student B: Yes, here it is.

Odd one out

103 Classwork or groupwork. Four pictures are shown and the students are asked to say which is the one which does not belong with the others.

Student: The cat is the odd one out.
Teacher: Why?
Student: Because it is an animal and the other pictures are machines.

104 **Variation** The students are encouraged to argue that a less obvious picture is the odd one out.
Student: The bicycle is the odd one out.
Teacher: Why?
Student: Because the cat has four legs, and the tractor and the bus have four wheels, but the bicycle only has two wheels!

What was their grouping?

105 Groupwork. Two groups work together, for example, two groups of four students. For this activity there must be twice as many pictures as there are students involved, for example, sixteen pictures for eight students. The pictures can be small and should be of a wide variety of objects. Each group is given half the number of pictures, i.e. eight pictures. The groups study their pictures and then choose about half of them which relate to a theme. The theme could be obvious, for example, foods, or it could be more subtle, for example, all the objects were invented in the last hundred years.

Each student then becomes responsible for a picture and studies it before being paired with a student from the other group. The two students try to find out as much as possible about each other's picture through questioning. Then the students return to their group and tell the other students in their group what they have found out about their partner's picture. Each group then tries to guess at the theme which the other group had decided on.

Desert island

106 Pairwork. The teacher displays a number of pictures of objects and animals, and tells the students that they have been shipwrecked on a desert island with just enough time to save six objects and/or animals from the ship before it sinks. Pairs of students look at the pictures and decide what they will save and what they will use it for. The pairs of students then divide up and form new pairs. The students then explain to each other what they decided to save and why.

107 **Variation** Instead of a desert island, the teacher can ask the students to choose objects for a stay in hospital, a camping holiday in Scotland, crossing the Sahara, a world tour by balloon, etc.

Word trees

108 Classwork. A picture is shown to the class. Students call out words which they associate with the picture, and these words are written on the board in groups according to their meaning. Groupings can be semantic or linguistic. For example, groupings for a picture of a street might be shops: baker's, grocer's, etc., or transport: bus, car, bicycle, etc.

4.5   Challenge to sequence

The students can be challenged to put various bits of information into a sequence. This sequence may be objective, for example, the stages in a process (ploughing, planting, fertilising, etc.); recipes; industrial processes; what to do in case of a road accident; what to do when someone faints, etc. Alternatively, the sequencing can be subjective, as in storytelling. Sometimes we can 'challenge' other people to tell stories; sometimes, of course, we might encourage them to do so and give them the 'opportunity' to do so. In this sense the activities described below could be listed under 'Opportunities' (see p. 000). However, for convenience, all ideas for promoting storytelling are described in this section.

Some teachers are firmly of the opinion that students should be given the time and encouragement to speak and write extensively without too much control and without too much stress on accuracy. These teachers believe that the skill of writing and speaking fluently and extensively can only be built up by giving confidence, a sense of purpose and an emphasis on meaning rather than on formal accuracy. Other teachers believe that fluency can only be built up by the students developing a firm and accurate grasp of a limited number of structures. Most of the activities described in the following section can be adapted for use by teachers who like to build up their students slowly to free composition as well as by those who believe in 'throwing the students in at the deep end'.

Gapped text

109 Individual or pairwork. The students are given a text with gaps in it. They complete the text by referring to a picture.

Jumbled sentences

110 Individual or pairwork. Jumbled sentences are given to the students. They write them out in the correct order, guided by a sequence of pictures.

Relevant sentences

111 Individual or pairwork. The students are given a sequence of pictures and several sentences. The students choose the sentences they think are relevant and base a story or description on them.

Change some words

112 Individual or pairwork. A text, a sequence of pictures and a number of alternative words for some of those in the text are given to the students. They write out the text with their choice of words, guided by reference to the pictures.

Adapt the story

113 Individual or pairwork. The students are given a story together with a list of words and phrases and a sequence of pictures. The students write out the story and add in any of the words and phrases they think will enrich the story. Alternatively, the students are given a basic story which they rewrite enriching it in any way they wish based on the series of pictures.

Question stories

114 Individual or pairwork. A sequence of questions is asked relating to a picture or a series of pictures. The students' answers to the questions guide them when writing a story or description.

Adapt a model story

115 Individual or pairwork. A text is given to the students which acts as a model. The students write another similar one by changing parts of it, perhaps in response to a different picture.

Story line

116 Individual or pairwork. A story line and some key points in the story are given to the students together with useful sentence pattern tables and a list of useful vocabulary and one or more pictures. The students then write a story.

Missing part

117 Individual or pairwork. The students are given a story with the beginning, the middle or the end missing. The students write out the given text and add in the missing part, based on one or more pictures.

Point of view

118 Individual or pairwork. A text is given to the students which is written from one person's point of view. The students rewrite the story from another person's point of view, basing it on one or more pictures.

Picture guided story

119 Individual or pairwork. A sequence of pictures or picture symbols is given and the students write the story without any other assistance or guidance.

Alphabetical order

120 Classwork or groupwork. The students see a number of pictures, name them and put them into alphabetical order.

121 **Variation** The students think of as many words connected with a picture as possible and then put the words into groups and then each group into alphabetical order.

Picture strip sequences

122 Pairwork or groupwork. The well-established way of promoting storytelling, descriptive writing or writing about processes is to give

the students a picture strip sequence. The picture strips devised specially for language teaching are usually very boring. Alternative sources are cartoon strips or photo story strips.

Note The students can be asked to write in the speech bubbles as well as write out a full text.

Describe and sequence

123 Groupwork. For a group of four students there should be four different pictures which together illustrate a story. Each student in the group is given one of the pictures, which he or she must not show to anyone else. Each student then describes his or her picture; the others can ask questions. The aim is to try to imagine everyone's picture and then to work out the sequence of the pictures in order to illustrate a story (or a process). If the pictures are intended for storytelling, the teacher must be clear as to whether there is a specific story for the students to find or whether it is an opportunity for inventing a story.

124 Variation A picture from a sequence is given to a group rather than to an individual. Students from each group go to other groups to ask them about their picture and then report back again. In this way each group gets to know all the pictures and can work out a probable sequence.

125 Variation Picture sequences can be chosen by the teacher to highlight certain language features, for example, the present simple tense. Having sorted out the order, the students can be asked to write down what the person does every day: wakes up, has breakfast, etc.

126 Variation The students illustrate and write their own picture strip sequences, including writing speech bubbles and the text below. One procedure is for a group to choose a known and liked story, for example, a currently popular film or television series. The students in the group then take one character from it and imagine him or her visiting the district of the school or college. The students discuss the sort of things which he or she might do. If this is done by the class as a whole, the teacher can write the ideas on the blackboard. The students then work together to produce a picture strip. When the strips are ready they can be exhibited, photocopied and distributed, read by other classes, reproduced in school or college journals.

Leslie H. launching a new Oil tanker.

73

Part B Emphasis on speaking and writing

Hold up picture story

127 Classwork. A sequence of pictures illustrating a story or a process is shown to the class by the teacher, out of order. The class discuss and decide where each picture should be placed in the sequence. A student is asked to stand at the front of the class and to hold up one of the pictures. The class then decide whether the next picture comes before or after it, and another student holds it up and stands in the appropriate position. Each student then writes up the story.

Picture story sequence

128 Classwork and groupwork. One student is asked to draw a simple drawing of someone on the board and the other students are asked to imagine the beginning of a story. Another student adds something to the drawing, perhaps a doorway, and the rest of the class suggest how the story might continue. One of the suggestions is chosen and the story is repeated from the beginning each time, guided by the drawings.

Note The teacher can ask questions in order to develop and enrich the story if it is rather ordinary. For example, the teacher might ask, 'How does he feel? Is he happy or unhappy, or angry?'

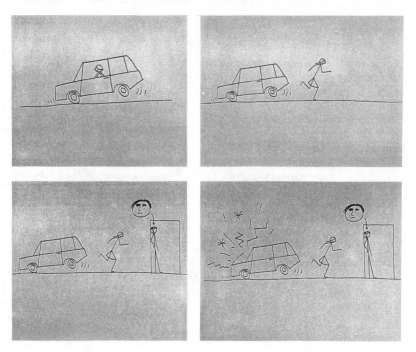

74

The first drawings have been partially erased and new parts begun.

The story might be: 'Suddenly, a car stopped. A woman got out of the car and began to run away. A man stood in a doorway. He had curly hair and dark eyebrows . . . '

129 **Variation** The teacher draws a picture on the board. The students must ask the teacher questions to find out the story that the teacher has in mind. As they establish each stage of the story the teacher draws another picture. He or she may decide not to speak, but merely confirms by nodding the head and starting the next drawing.

Note At the end of this activity the students can be asked to write up the story either as it was devised by the class or as they think it should have been devised.

Four picture story

130 Individual and pairwork. The teacher shows a picture to the class and tells the students that they have four minutes to start writing a story based on it. After four minutes students take it in turns to read their story to their neighbour. The teacher asks one or two students to read their stories out to the whole class. Then the teacher shows the class another picture and tells the students to continue the same story as before but now referring to the new picture. After four minutes the teacher stops the students and they read the continuation of their stories to their neighbours. This is repeated for three or four pictures. (Adapted from Alan Maley and Alan Duff, *Drama Techniques in Language Learning*.)

Abstract story sequence

131 Pairwork. The teacher asks a student to draw an abstract picture on the board. Working in pairs, the students begin to write a story based on the picture. After four minutes pairs take it in turns to read their stories to another pair. The teacher then asks another student to add another abstract drawing and the students then continue the same story, referring to the new picture. Pairs of students read the continuation of their story to the same pair. At each 'reading' stage the teacher can ask one or two students to read out their story to the whole class.

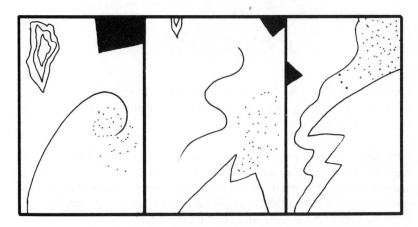

1. I tried to avoid the crowd of people. I walked around them. I was frightened. Then I saw Hannah. I ran into the crowd but I couldn't find her.

2. I lost Hannah and I lost my way. The crowd were shouting. The tank moved away. I dicided to stay with the crowd

3. Then we knew that we were trapped. We were caught between the river and the sea. The tank waited for us. Three brave people strode forwards.

Flowchart of shapes

132 Classwork and pairwork. The teacher draws a flowchart on the board similar to the one illustrated below. At each stage of drawing the flow-chart the teacher can ask the students what sort of emotion the shapes might represent, and then what sort of situations the emotions might arise out of. Students, working in pairs, devise stories based on the different shapes and guided by the connecting lines. Pairs of students take it in turns to read their stories to each other.

133 **Variation** Pairs of students exchange the stories they have written. They should read each other's stories and then try to find which route the other pair took through the flowchart.

Note Magazine pictures can be used as well as or instead of abstract shapes.

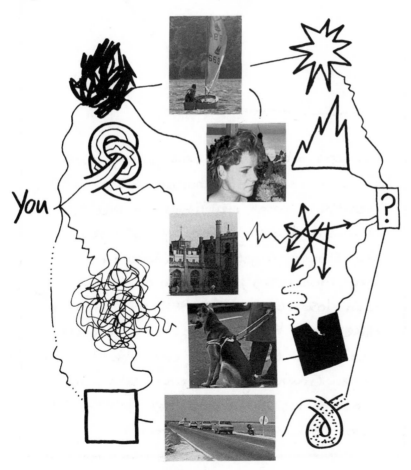

Line stories

134 Classwork and individual work. A line or several lines are drawn on the board. The students imagine that each line represents a person's life or a series of circumstances affecting a person. The line intersections could be interpreted as the times when the people meet.

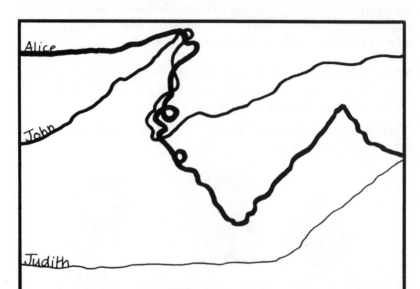

Alice was a happy, confident young woman. She was a professional woman of the 1980's. Everything went well until she met John. It was a disaster for both of them! They stayed together for a long time but they quarrelled, they became ill and they both lost their jobs. At last John left Alice and his life began to improve. But Alice became ill and she lost all hope. Gradually, however, she improved and things began to get better. But it was only for a short time ... .

Structured stories

35 Groups of three. The teacher structures the students' stories in eight stages.

1. Working together, the students choose three main characters for their story. The teacher can give the students a list of characters to choose from. Each student is then responsible for one character.

2. The students choose a shape to represent the nature of each of their characters:

  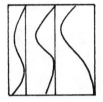

3. The students decide on four things about each of their characters:

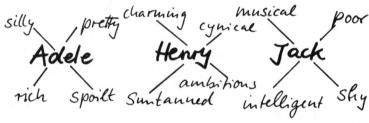

These four things can be good or bad. They can be physical or personality features of the character or material objects related to the character.

4. The students fill in the chart below to describe their characters more fully:

	3	2	1	0	1	2	3	
honest		J			A		H	dishonest
wise		J	H				A	foolish
kind	J			H	A			unkind
selfless		J					HA	selfish
generous		J			H		A	greedy
lively	H				J	A		boring
careful		J	H				A	careless

5. The students work together to produce a total of six pictures (drawings or magazine pictures), each on a piece of card. The pictures can be of a place, an object or a person, but not any of the protagonists.

6. The cards are arranged so that each picture represents a stage in the story in the following sequence: Goal, Problem, Opening situation, Journey and difficulties overcome, Turning point, Outcome.
7. Each student then writes a story based on the three characters but from the point of view of his or her character.
8. They read out their completed stories to each other.

(Adapted from A. B. Hansen, K. Jones, M. Legutke, 'Interactive approaches to fiction'.)

Word and action

136 Classwork. In this activity the class invents the story but the teacher tells it for them.

The teacher shows the class a picture and asks for any ideas which could begin a story. The students offer ideas and the teacher combines their ideas to start a story. He or she then shows another picture and asks for a development of the story. The teacher may tell the class that whatever the students suggest must be incorporated into the story, and this applies even if the information is contradictory. For example, if one student says the person is 40 and the other that they are 50 the teacher must accept these two facts and ask the class how to incorporate them into the story. For example, 'She's 50 years old, but she is so careful with herself that she looks as if she is 40'. The teacher is responsible for asking questions and for constantly retelling the story and then incorporating new suggestions into it. The students only have to call out as they get an idea. Thus the students feel that they are inventing a long and complicated story but the actual linguistic demands on them are not great. Even the least able students can contribute something and hear their contribution being continually reused. (Adapted from 'Word and Action'.)

Note The story can be written up afterwards; some students may like to add illustrations.

Silent teacher story

37 Classwork. The class invent a story which the teacher must illustrate as it is invented. The class must make sure they help the teacher to illustrate the story satisfactorily. The teacher does not speak at any time, except to explain that the class will be responsible and that he or she will not help them. Some teachers make a lot of use of this 'silent technique' and their classes become used to it and are very quick to realise what they have to do.

Picture story dominoes

138 Groupwork. Each student is given five small pictures (all the pictures should be the same size and mounted on card). The students take it in turns to put down a picture next to one already on the table. If the student can continue the story referring to the new picture then it can be left there. If he or she can't continue then the picture must be taken back again.

An example of a story:
Harold was a cheerful, happy man who loved flowers.
He always took flowers to his mother. She was in hospital because she had fallen off her horse.
She used to ride in the mountains .....

Dungeons and dragons

139 Classwork. This activity is based on the internationally known type of game sometimes called 'Dungeons and Dragons'. In this variation the teacher has worked out a landscape in his or her mind. The teacher tells the class that they are all at one point which he or she marks with a cross on the blackboard (no picture or map on it at this stage). The teacher tells the class that he or she represents all their senses but not their intelligence, and that he or she can tell them what they can see, hear, smell, taste and touch if they ask for the information, but can't advise them what to do. Their aim is to escape from the landscape. The teacher tells them what they can see, hear, touch, etc. The students discuss what they should do when faced with a river, or with a dragon, etc.

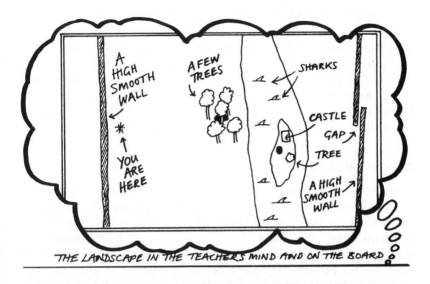

THE LANDSCAPE IN THE TEACHER'S MIND AND ON THE BOARD

Here is one complete landscape which the teacher might have in his or her mind, together with the state of the drawing on the board after a class has managed to establish some of the landscape and to travel in it (adapted from a landscape drawn by Rhodri Jones during a teachers' workshop). It is annotated with the sort of information which the teacher would offer if the class asked for it. The route shown is what most groups choose to take in order to 'escape' from the landscape. As the students move through the landscape the teacher marks their route, and also draws in the objects, etc. which the students see.

Note It is possible to do this activity with large groups of students if they are involved and motivated enough to take part. Sometimes the students split up into smaller groups to explore different parts of the landscape. The teacher must never be tempted to give advice. He or she should only say, 'What would you like to know?' 'What are you going to do now?' 'Are you all going to do that or are some of you going to stay where you are or do something else?' Experience shows that an upper-intermediate to advanced proficiency group of students takes about half an hour to get out of the landscape!

Numbered picture stories

140 Groupwork. The teacher displays about twenty pictures around the room. The pictures could be a mixture of people, objects and places, or alternatively they could all show objects. They could be pinned on the walls or laid on desks and each picture should have a number on it. The aim is for students, working in twos or threes, to devise a story based on the pictures. The pictures can be used in any order but they must all be incorporated in some way. The students are given a time limit and are not allowed to make notes on their story, but must remember it. When they have prepared their story (and this may mean going through it several times in order to get it right) they then tell their story to another group who ensure that all the pictures are used.

Newspaper photographs

141 Individual work. Each student is given a photograph taken from a newspaper or magazine. He or she must think of a caption to the picture and write an article with a headline. Afterwards the student can be shown the actual caption, article and headline for comparison.

142 **Variation** Pairs write a story and a caption. They then exchange their photo and caption (but not their story) with another pair. The other pair must then write a new story, guided by the picture and the caption they have received.

Single picture stories

143 Pairwork and classwork. Each pair of students is given a picture of a place or a person. The pictures should be evocative and interesting. The students must study their picture and try to imagine everything they can about it and then write a description. The pictures and the written descriptions are then collected and displayed. Each picture is given a number and each description a letter. Everyone then reads the descriptions and tries to match them up with the pictures, making

notes of the numbers of the pictures and the letters of the descriptions which seem to match.

44 Variation A picture of a scene and/or incident. The students write a description of what they think took place just before the time in the picture and a second one about what they think will happen after the time in the picture. All the descriptions are displayed and everyone tries to match the texts and pictures together.

45 Variation A picture of a person. Students write a letter as if they were a person in one picture to a person in another picture.

Detective story

46 Pairwork. Photocopies of objects of various kinds plus maps and pictures of people and places are displayed. The display can be random or the objects might be grouped and labelled as having been discovered at certain places on the maps. These photocopies represent detectives' evidence. The students must try to imagine what the connection between the objects might be and write up a detective's report or idea of what might have occurred.

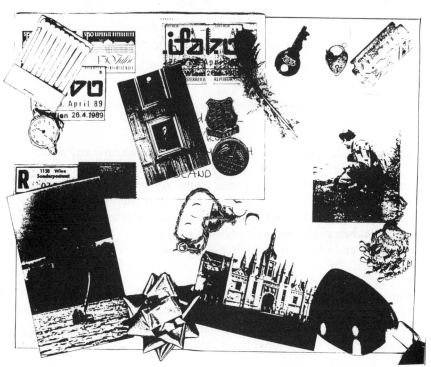

Picture maps

147 Pairwork. Each pair is given a picture map, which might be of a city popular with tourists.

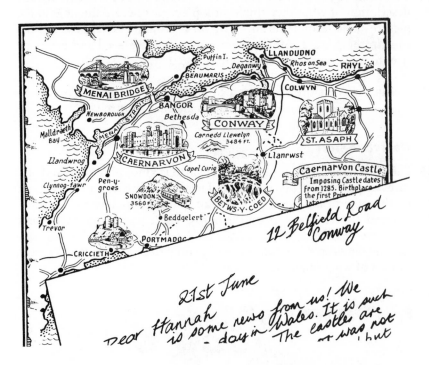

The students are asked to plan a day in the city and to write a letter home about it.

148 **Variation** The students are given a map of a landscape and asked to plan a walk or car journey through it. Students then exchange plans and follow each other's proposed route. Alternatively, the students plan a route and then write an account as if they have walked or driven along it, saying which way they went and what they saw. The students then exchange their account with another pair, who follow the route and check to see if any other places of interest could have been seen.

149 **Variation** Groupwork. Two drawings recording a street accident are prepared. Each drawing is different from the other in certain respects and represents the view of a different witness. Students work in groups of four. The groups are divided into pairs and each pair studies

Communication and challenges

a different drawing and then writes an account of the accident from the point of view of their witness. When the accounts have been written the students compare them to see what the differences are.

Group sequence stories

150 Groupwork. Each group is given a picture. Each group writes two sentences about its picture before passing it on to the next group. Each group then studies the new picture and adds two more sentences to the story based on the new picture. When the pictures have passed through all the groups, the stories are displayed and compared.

New group stories

151 Groupwork. Each group is given a picture. Each group writes two sentences about the picture which could be part of a story, and then each student in the group copies down the two sentences. New groups are now formed, made up of one student from each of the first groups. Thus each of the pictures is represented in each of the new groups, and each student has a copy of the two sentences written by his or her first group. The new groups now try to put all the sentences into an order which could tell a story. They can modify the sentences and they can link them by using various devices, such as connectors, pronouns, etc.

Picture and picture symbol sequences

152 Pair, group or classwork. It is possible to represent stories almost entirely without words by means of pictures and picture symbols. The students are shown the sequences and asked to guess at the story and its details. The story unfolds, therefore, without the need to rely on verbal prompting, and, of course, students can be asked to compose their own picture sequence stories. Enthusiasts of this technique say that it is successful because it stimulates the students and makes them search actively for meaning. They say that the students learn a range of basic picture symbols rapidly and without confusion. Some teachers wonder whether the need to learn a range of picture symbols is not just another burden on the students' ability and goodwill.

The technique is so close to ancient approaches to writing that it can hardly be called new! However, recently, a comprehensive focus on the technique has been developed and a 'grammar' of picture symbols has been invented (William Chuckney, *The Skeleton System*). The system makes use of over 150 picture symbols.

D

Example:

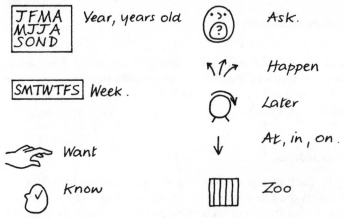

HERE ARE SOME OF CHUCKNEY'S PICTURE SYMBOLS
REPRODUCED WITH PERMISSION

The picture story is based on picture symbols which must be learned and pictures whose purpose can be guessed at.

Example:

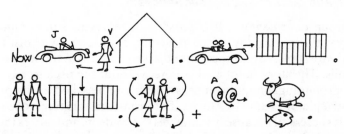

THE BEGINNING OF A STORY
SKELETON 3

Now Jane is picking Vi up. They are driving to the zoo together. Now they are at the zoo. They are walking around and they are looking at the animals.

It is tempting for word-centred people to feel that such a method is distracting and difficult. In fact, many people are visually gifted and spend much of their school and college life without the opportunity to make use of their ability. Teachers with an interest in this technique find it a rewarding approach and one which can allow students who are normally under-achievers to shine.

4.6   Challenge to order

In the activities in this section the students are asked to place a number of pictures in order of quality. Their judgement of the qualities of the pictures can be objective or subjective. Each of the activities can be extended by carrying out a class survey, gathering and grouping the information. In this way class norms and individual variations can be compared and discussed. It is the discussion which is of particular value for language development.

The best fruit

153   Pairwork and classwork. A wall picture or a number of separate pictures of fruit are shown to the students. The students are asked to say which fruit would be the best to take on a school trip (objective) or to put the fruits in their own order of preference (subjective).

The best food

154   Pairwork and classwork. Various pictures of food are displayed. The students work together in pairs to decide which are the healthiest foods and which the least healthy. The pairs then argue their points of view in a class discussion.

The best colour

155   Pairwork and classwork. The students are asked to discuss in pairs which colours would be best and which least successful for a variety of purposes: road safety jackets for road workers, shop front colours for chemists/hairdressers/banks, etc. (Or they are asked to put the colours in their own order of preference.) A survey can then be made of the class as a whole and compared with the preferences in other classes.

The best holiday

156 Individual work and classwork. The students are shown a number of pictures representing different types of holiday. They are asked to say which ones they would prefer and which they wouldn't like.

157 **Variation** Students are asked to suggest which would be the most and which the least suitable holiday places for other students in the class. They can then compare their suggestions with what the other students actually chose for themselves.

The best painting

158 Classwork. A number of reproductions of paintings are displayed, and the students are asked to say which would be the most suitable and which the least suitable to hang in: a school staff room, a school corridor, a hospital ward, a business reception area, a hotel lounge, a youth club. Then individual students are asked to say which paintings they would like to have at home.

The best advertisement

159 Pairwork and classwork. A number of advertisements are displayed, and pairs are asked to evaluate their relative effectiveness. A class discussion can then follow.

160 **Variation** The evaluation of advertisements is carried out with particular people in mind. For example, four pictures of people are displayed so that all the class can see them. Then a variety of advertisements are displayed and the students, working in pairs, decide which advertisements would be attractive to each of the four people. A survey of rankings can be written on the board.

161 **Variation** Pairwork. Each pair is given an advertisement picture and then writes ten sentences on ten separate bits of paper about the product. Some sentences should be true, some possible and some impossible. Then student A keeps the ten sentences and student B joins another student A. Student B must now try to arrange the other pair's sentences into: true, possible, and impossible.

4.7 Challenge to memorise

Challenging people's memories and ability to memorise is the basis for a number of well-known games. The ability to remember is, of course, a key factor in successful language learning: the activities in this section contribute not only to the remembering of words but, more significantly, to general techniques for improving memory.

Kim's game

162 Classwork and pairwork. About ten objects are shown to the students for around twenty seconds. The objects can be real, on picture cards or on an overhead projector. After twenty seconds the pictures are covered up or hidden from the students. The students ust then try to remember each one. They can be asked to do this by first of all writing down the names of the objects they remember and then comparing their list with a neighbour's list.

163 **Variation** Each student writes down as much as he or she can remember about the pictures and then exchanges their writing with their neighbour. The teacher then asks students what their neighbour wrote about each object and to say whether they agree or not. After discussion with various students, the teacher shows the pictures.

164 **Variation** Each pair is given some pictures or a single complicated picture to study. Then each pair exchanges pictures with another pair and they take it in turns to test each others' memories.

165 **Variation** Two similar pictures are shown one after the other. The students try to remember the differences between them.

Note 1 To practise number and plural forms: the pictures should include several of the same or a similar object, for example, cars.

Note 2 To practise adjectives: there should be several similar objects which can only be differentiated by the use of adjectives, including comparative forms.

Note 3 To practise language for particular 'fields': pictures of objects from the same class of objects can be shown, for example, forms of transport; for containers the pictures can show boxes, parcels, tubes, etc.

Note 4 To practise the use of the present perfect: the teacher and students draw various objects or people on the board. The students try to remember them and then close their eyes and place their heads on their arms. While the students have their eyes closed the teacher or another student makes changes to the drawings on the board. The class must then say what has been changed.

Teacher: What have I done?

Student: You've made the man's nose longer.

Remembering a scene

166 Classwork or groupwork. The teacher or student looks at a large wall picture carefully and then stands with his or her back to it. He or she then tries to describe the picture from memory. The class can see the picture and are allowed to ask questions. This activity can also be done by asking the students if they can remember what is behind them in the classroom or what it is possible to see from the front door of the school.

Eyewitness

167 Classwork. The teacher discusses the reliability of eyewitnesses. He or she then shows the class a picture for several seconds, for example, a street scene. Students say what they saw: what was in the street, what was happening, what people looked like, etc. The students compare what they remember and if appropriate, argue their case.

Note The picture may be a slide which is projected for a few moments or a small picture which the teacher shows to the class by walking slowly between the students.

168 **Variation** Pairwork. The teacher has a picture. Student A in each pair comes up and looks at the teacher's picture and then returns to student B. Student A describes the picture to student B who writes down what A says and then tries to draw a picture of it. Student A tries to help B to do this. Finally, all the students compare what they have written and drawn with the original.

169 **Variation** Pairwork and groupwork. Students in pairs write down a description of what they remember in the picture. Then each pair joins another pair and the group now compare and combine their descriptions. Two groups now join (to make about eight students) and compare and combine descriptions. The teacher then asks one student from each group to read out their group's description. All the descriptions are compared and then, finally, compared with the picture.

Remembering a route

170 Classwork. The teacher shows a large 'bird's eye' view of a landscape or townscape. The teacher traces his or her finger across the landscape. The students try to remember which route the teacher took and then retell what he or she did and saw on the journey.

Note Published pictures like this are rare. However, such pictures are not difficult to draw. They can be produced as part of another activity by the students themselves. Instead of using a picture, a map of a town, region, country or a world map could be used.

ADVICE: DRAW THE ROADS FIRST!

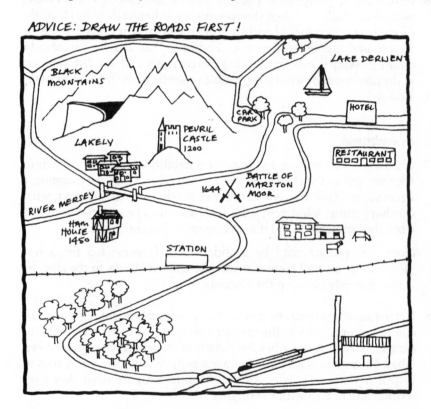

Pelmanism

171 Groupwork. For each group there should be ten pairs of cards, which should all be the same size. The pairs might be two pictures which relate together, for example, cow/calf; or a picture and a text, for example, a picture of a cow and the word 'cow'; or the pair could be pictures of the same kind of object but different examples (two different types of car); or the pair could be of identical pictures.

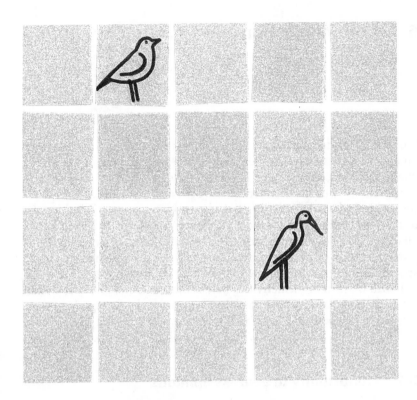

The students in the group examine all the pictures. The cards are then shuffled so the pairs are no longer together and laid in a neat pattern, face down, on the table. The students take it in turns to point to the backs of two cards and say what the picture and/or text is. If the student has remembered (or guessed!) correctly and the two cards make a pair, then he or she can keep them.

Remembering a sequence

72 Classwork and pairwork. The teacher tells a story illustrated by a number of picture cards which are shown to the class and then propped up, for example, on the board shelf. The teacher then turns the pictures to face the board. On the back of each picture card there is a number. Students, working in pairs, try to remember the story, making written notes related to each number. Then the class reconstruct the story orally, discussing and then agreeing on a final version. The teacher then turns the pictures to face the class and rereads the original story so that it can be compared with the class's version.

5   Communication and opportunities

Sometimes students need an opportunity to investigate a subject, or an opportunity to express their feelings about a subject, rather than a challenge. Of course, there is an overlap between 'challenge' and 'opportunity' but the distinction is worth making as it leads to a different kind of work. Activities based on an 'opportunity' tend to take much longer than the various 'challenge' activities of the previous chapter. The activities described below are usually experienced as part of a study of a subject area; any subject area which interests the students and involves language is of value in language teaching.

It will be seen in the activities below that students of any level can study at least some aspects of a topic through the foreign language. Furthermore, activities can be linguistically controlled, partly controlled or open and might involve any or all of the skills.

5.1   Opportunity to express opinions

Juxtaposing pictures

Many topics can be discussed by the simple idea of displaying a number of pictures (and texts) which represent different aspects of the topic. By juxtaposing the pictures their different qualities are highlighted. Students respond differently to the implied relationships between the information in the pictures and there are consequently 'opinion gaps' and reasons for speaking.

In the example here, types of job are considered. Other topics which can be readily represented in this way include: types of holiday, forms of transport, foods, sports and hobbies. Less well-established topics might include: the psychology of imagery, the psychology of buying and selling, changes in daily life through history.

173   Classwork. The students are shown a number of pictures (four to eight) which represent various aspects of different jobs. Aspects might include: physical or mental strain, whether they are outside or inside, alone or with others, well paid or badly paid. The students are asked to consider the advantages and disadvantages of the various jobs and to say which they would prefer and why.

96

5.2 Opportunity to express experiences and feelings

Pictures in the mind

Most people can see pictures in their mind. Some people see them more readily than others and some cannot see any images at all. Looking at the images and trying to describe them to a neighbour is a demanding task but also a fruitful one in terms of the use of language.

As not everyone can see pictures readily it is advisable to carry out this activity in two stages, first of all describing a picture for the students to see in their imagination and then asking the students if they can see a picture without any help. Most people can manage the first stage.

74 Pairwork and classwork. The teacher asks the students to close their eyes and then describes a scene slowly to them. For example, 'There is a horse standing on top of a small hill. The hill is grassy. The grass is long and it is waving in the breeze. The horse is white and it is standing sideways to us. Its mane and its tail are waving in the breeze, just like the grasses are waving', etc.

Working in pairs the students discuss whether they saw what the teacher described and try to find out if there were any differences. For example, 'Was the sky blue or cloudy?' The students then discuss what they saw with the teacher and the class as a whole.

Once the students have tried to imagine the teacher's description they take it in turns to look at the pictures in their minds and then to describe what they can see to their neighbour.

Note Looking at pictures in the mind is a particularly sensitive activity and one which each teacher will know how to present to her or his individual classes.

Imagining

175 Classwork. When a blackboard or whiteboard has been cleaned it is covered with smears, rubbings, marks and spots (unless it has been washed). The students are invited to say what animals, objects or scenes they imagine they can see on the board. Then individual students are asked to come to the board to point out and describe what they can see.

176 **Variation** Any 'splodge' of ink or paint can be used to promote speculation and imagination in the same way.

177 **Variation** Any shapes like cracks on the ceiling, flaking plaster, clouds or the foliage of trees may also be used.

Pictures and feelings

178 Individual work, groupwork and classwork. The teacher (or the students) makes an exhibition of reproductions of paintings either by mounting them on the walls of the classroom or laying them on desks. Students first of all have a look at each picture, then they decide which picture they connect with a happy moment in their lives, which with an unhappy moment and which with a stressful moment. They make notes on these impressions. Then, sitting in groups, the students explain their personal connections with the paintings.

179 **Variation** Pairwork. The students tell each other where they would place each of the pictures if they could. For example, 'I would put the Turner picture in our sitting room at home.' 'I would put the Mondrian picture in my bedroom.' The students can ask each other to give reasons for their ideas, for example, 'I would put it there because it is so calm.'

Caged in a stone

trapped   sea   stone   Deak   creature   Last bird in the ~~br~~ world
                                                                    alone

egg   Dird   Cry

night   darkness   Cm cry against the light

Pool of night   Cm cry against
                  the dying of the light

Leaving this doorway   wom None a black dewdrop

from the w...   ...ht ~~trapped~~ in that   Screaming silently

A hatching   Facing the world
                                alone

the egg of n...   black dewdrop

trapped in th...   in a frozen spring

a deep beake...   sea stone

silent so...   rolled in ebb
                and flow

Bird

Is this a bird hatching
From the egg of night?

Or

Is this the last bird in the world
Looking for the last man
In order to peck out
His brains,
Caged in a sea rolled stone,
A deep beaked moan defying
The dying of the light?

Pictures and poetry

180 Classwork and pairwork. The teacher projects a slide or displays a wall picture which has a powerful emotional quality. A reproduction of a painting or a quality photograph of artistic worth provide good starting points. It is helpful if the picture is not easy to interpret so that a variety of responses can be stimulated.

The students should first of all discuss what they can see in the picture and then how they interpret what they can see and finally how they feel about it. The students may then work by themselves, in pairs or in small groups. They should begin by writing down words for the key aspects of the picture which they feel are significant. Once these words are written down, the students should add other words and phrases to the key words, each time thinking of the aspects which interest them. Finally, the students write a poem making use of the ideas and the language they have collected.

181 **Variation** A lot of pictures of different subjects are displayed. The selection can include pictures which have a powerful emotional content and feeling but may also include pictures of more mundane subjects. The students are invited to select several pictures and to base their poem on them.

Personal picture collages

182 Individual, pairwork and classwork. The students are invited to make a collage about themselves. This is a particularly useful activity for a new class of students as they can get to know each other quickly in this way. The collage can be made of pictures they cut out of magazines, their own pictures, their own drawings, texts cut from magazines, etc. or real things which can be stuck down, for example, tickets for the theatre. The students put their names on the back of the collage.

The students prepare to speak about themselves, their interests and concerns: they may have to use the dictionary or refer to the teacher for help. Then all the collages are displayed and students try to guess who each collage represents. After this, students work in pairs. Each student studies the other, writing down a profile based on the collage and what each part of it means. Then, in a general session, each student introduces his or her partner and talks about them. Other students may ask questions.

183 **Variation** Collages can be done on particular places, people or ideas. The students can also be asked to write a text to go with the collage.

101

184 Variation Collages can be done by pairs or even by groups of students working together.

Note Of course, any type of picture can be used as a starting point for the exchange of personal experiences; it does not need to be a collage.

Personal drawings

185 Individual and classwork. It should be emphasised that the students do not need to be talented artists in order to be able to carry out this activity. Nor does the teacher need to be an art teacher! The students are asked to make a drawing and write a short text to go with it.

Various subjects can be set, for example: What I would like to do one day; What I do everyday; What I really like doing; A poem; Fantasy animals, what they do and what they are like.

(Adapted from Sharon Bassano and Mary Ann Christison, *Drawing Out*.)

This is a picture of one of my earliest memorys. It is a picture of my dad pushing a lawn mower. It was at my Grandmas cottage in wales about seven year ago.

Tim Greed

Greetings cards

186 Individual work. Students design, illustrate and write greetings cards. These cards should be sent off to 'real' people so that there is a sense of purpose and the chance of an actual reply! Cards might be designed for festivals, for greetings, for best wishes, for success in examinations, for recovery from illness or for general 'cheering up' cards.

Picture memories

187 Individual, pairwork and classwork. Students try to remember the appearance of places familiar to them, for example, their front door. Do they remember it from outside or inside? Do they remember the colour, the design of the handle, etc.? Students first of all think about the image, perhaps drawing it and making notes about it. Then they show it to their neighbour and discuss it. Finally, the students' experiences of trying to remember are discussed.

188 **Variation** The teacher asks what the students can remember of the view from the front door of the college or school or alternatively, what they can remember of the back of the classroom.

189 **Variation** Students try to remember and describe people who they are close to, or who they all know.

Art and design

There are various aspects of art which can be studied and explored without the support of a professional teacher of art. The activities described below investigate the qualities of lines, shapes and pictorial symbols. The activities are language based: they invite exploration, expression and communication through language and in this sense they are of potential value to the language learner.

Expressive lines

190 Individual, pairwork and classwork. The lines below are shown to the students. Individually, they write down words which they think describe the emotional feelings of the lines. The teacher could give the students a range of words to choose from or leave it open to the students to make use of words they know. Students compare their interpretations in pairs and then with the rest of the class. Differences are discussed, and the idea of synonyms and similarity of meaning is established, for example, 'sad', 'miserable', 'unhappy'.

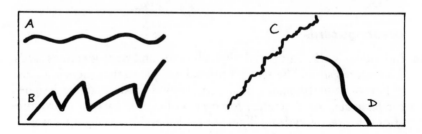

The activity can be extended by comparing the words chosen by students in the class with the results of research done with 500 people, in which line A was described by the majority as 'happy' (or a similar word), line B as 'angry', line C as 'excited', and line D as 'sad' (with acknowledgements to Lundholm, Poffenburger and Barrows).

191 **Variation** Students working together look through magazine pictures of clothes, cars, house furniture and decoration as well as paintings. They try to find examples of the expressive lines, which they discuss. The teacher then asks one student from each pair to change with a student from another pair. The 'visiting' student must then try to find out through discussion what connection has been made by the first pair of students between the lines and the pictures selected.

Shapes in design

192 Individual, pairwork and classwork. The teacher shows the students the shapes below. The students write down which shapes they like best and which they like least. They then write down which shapes they would choose as decorative symbols for: (a) a firm of motor engineers; (b) a pop video recording company; (c) a book publisher; (d) a holiday firm; (e) a fast food company. Pairs of students work together explaining their choices. All the students then report on their choices and any general agreements are discussed.

Understanding pictorial symbols

193 Individual, pairwork and classwork. The signs below are shown to the students. Each student tries to imagine what the sign represents and writes down his or her interpretation. Students compare and discuss their interpretations first of all in pairs, then in groups and then in the class as a whole. The reasons why some signs are interpreted by many people in a similar way and some very differently are discussed. Students suggest how some of the designs could be improved.

Note 1 Picture symbols can sometimes be found in holiday brochures and road safety booklets.

Note 2 Designers give a lot of importance to the need to design symbols which can be understood by everyone. It is not easy to do and involves thinking hard about who is going to see the symbol and in what sort of situation. The students may like to discuss this.

Note 3 Students may like to discuss the relationship between the abstract appearance of a shape (as studied in the previous activity) and the way the shape represents a concept, for example, the British Rail symbol might be considered: (a) dynamic in its diagonal line and reliable in its horizontal lines; and (b); a representation of railway lines and junctions.

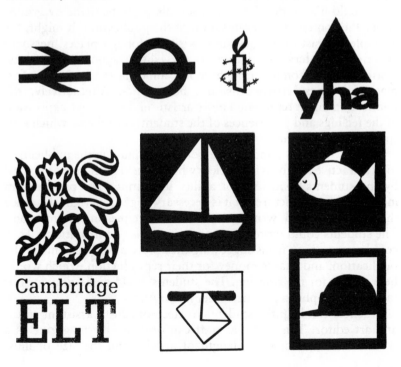

Part B Emphasis on speaking and writing

Thematic writing

Producing a class publication

In recent years teachers and students have begun to feel that there should be a reason for writing which is not only concerned with improving the students' English. There should be a sense of real purpose in writing for at least part of the time, and this sense of purpose means writing about things of personal importance for people other than the teacher.

One activity which some teachers have found very rewarding is to help the students produce a leaflet, a magazine or a book or to prepare an exhibition. The publication can be taken home, given to visitors to the school, college or local tourist information centre, sent to other schools or to pen pals. (I have received school magazines from the Canary Islands and Denmark.) Exhibitions can be seen by visitors to the school or college and by the students' families, as well as by other classes.

194 Individual, groupwork and classwork. A useful lesson can be spent analysing publications which the students think are relevant to the kind they would like to produce. They can begin to talk about what they would like to do. Written proposals could be made by groups about the content and organisation of the publication. It might, for example, consist of articles about visits to foreign places, personal experiences, interviews, letters to the editor, agony aunt letters, stories, poetry, comic strips, humour, amazing facts, useful information, recipes, crosswords and horoscopes. Alternatively, the publication might represent a more artistic and subjective expression of the feelings and experiences of the students on a theme which is of special interest to them.

Pictures will play a major role not only in making the publication look attractive but in giving variety when the text itself may be limited by the students' own level of ability in writing. The pictures can include magazine pictures (if it is necessary to get copyright clearance the students could write genuine letters requesting permission). The students could write to outside sources for contributions. They could also write to firms suggesting they place advertisements in the publication, and charge money for their reproduction, which would help to pay for the printing. The students could make drawings or take photographs to produce other illustrations.

Teachers can help the students to elect an editor, assistant editor and art editor. This editorial staff can organise the magazine as a whole, and determine the length of articles and the size of illustrations. They can be responsible for sticking down the articles and illustrations so that it can be reproduced. The writing is best done by small teams of students working together.

The publication can be reproduced in two ways: by photocopying or lithography. Lithography is expensive if only a few copies are produced, but it is not expensive if many are produced and a small fee is charged for each copy. If the school or college authorities think that the publication might be of interest to a wider audience, money might be found for it to be printed by lithography.

The activity of producing a publication can be simple (producing just a photocopied sheet) or a major project taking many weeks or even months. The idea of a major project might be impossible due to examination pressures in many schools. However, it should be appreciated by teachers that the wealth of reasons for speaking, listening, reading and writing in order to produce a publication more than justify the work and time involved.

Teachers who have produced publications with their students report that the students often undertake the work in their own time. They also report an improvement in relationships between teacher and students.

Note 1 The texts and pictures should be done in black rather than in a colour or a pale grey. Black reproduces easily and well.

Note 2 Themes undertaken by teachers and their students may include: a magazine about the school and current events; a leaflet about the school and its history and relationship with the community; a leaflet about the locality for foreign visitors which can be given to the local tourist office for distribution (it could be a specialist leaflet for young people); a leaflet for use in local museums and other places of local interest.

5.3   Opportunity to speculate and express opinions

It is possible to 'read' a picture if one can recognise the objects represented in it and then deduce what the relationship between them might be. The speculation might have no final answer; on the other hand there might be sufficient information for the student to deduce what is implied. Pictures chosen for 'speculation' must be ambiguous, and, most importantly, the teacher must not have a fixed interpretation of the picture. This would restrict the imaginations of the students! Students can be asked to speculate about the picture as observers or to imagine themselves as someone in the picture.

Examples of speculative activities described below are related to people, actions, places and objects. The pictures representing each of these subjects are chosen to present a problem of interpretation and identification.

Who is she?

195 Pairwork and classwork. Pairs discuss what they think about a picture (a projected slide or individual pictures for pairwork) and their interpretations are shared with the class. 'What sort of person is she?' 'How old is she?' 'Is she poor or quite well off?' 'What sort of job does she do?' 'How does she feel at this moment?' 'What sort of place is she in?' 'What might have happened?' 'What might be going to happen soon?'

196 **Variation** Students imagine what the person would be like as a friend, companion, relative, etc.

197 **Variation** The students are asked to imagine themselves as the person and they are then interviewed by other students in pairs or groups.

Note All of these activities encourage students to think about other people. They also raise the question of how far it is possible to know people merely from their appearance.

110

Where's this?

198 Pairwork. Each pair is given a postcard of a place. The students study the card and try to deduce what sort of place it is and write down their observations. (The teacher might discuss with the class what aspects to consider before starting the activity.) The students then exchange postcards with another pair and do the same again. After this, the pairs divide to form new pairs, and they now discuss what conclusions they came to.

What's this?

199 Pairwork and classwork. The students examine a picture of an object and decide what it is, what it might be used for, how valuable it is, where it is, who it might belong to, how important it is to that person, how they acquired it, etc. These and other associations can be discussed in pairs and then in groups or by the class as a whole.

Historical paintings

200 Classwork. Reproductions of paintings are displayed. Students speculate about the life of the times represented: the customs, the assumptions and ideas, the material objects and developments.

5.4 Opportunity to express and debate opinions

Investigating a topic

The topic approach, which has been such a familiar part of primary education for many years, has been developed in recent years by a number of teachers of older students. In principle, the topic approach means that the teacher and students study a single theme for a certain period of time. The students' language development arises out of their study of the theme through reading and listening and the communication of their findings and opinions through speaking and writing. Pictures can have an important role in some topics and that is the reason for including at least a reference to topic work in this book. The example given is the topic of advertising.

Advertising

201 Classwork, groupwork and pairwork. Advertising relies to a large extent on pictorial imagery. The imagery invites reading, personal reaction, differences of opinion, and therefore discussion. Further-

more, if foreign advertisements are used they will provide a source of cultural information. Clearly, advertising lends itself to project work in language learning.

Teachers who have built a project around advertising have followed these stages:

- Classwork. Discussing advertising in the students' own environment: what is advertised, where and how; restrictions; students' own feelings.
- Pairwork and classwork. Looking at persuasive advertisements: what they are trying to sell, who they are trying to sell to and how they are trying to persuade; the role of pictures, words, and images; men, women, animals, etc.; stereotyping; storytelling; associations.
- Pairwork and classwork. Looking at informative advertisements: what they are trying to achieve and for whom; whether the imagery and text are purely informative; whether the information is used for purposes of persuasion.
- Groupwork and classwork. Display of advertisements plus a written analysis.
- Groupwork and classwork. Creating an advertising campaign with ideas for advertisements in newspapers, on radio, TV and bill hoardings; displaying them.

Drugs. Die. Die. Die. Die. Die.
Drugs. Die. Die. Die. Die. Die.
Drugs. Die. Die. Die. Die. Die.
Dead! Dead! Dead! Dead!
Dead!

5.5   Opportunity to dramatise

Creating class soap operas

202   Classwork. Soap operas like 'Dallas' are known in many countries. Students are familiar with the characters and with their struggles, triumphs and failures. Students can create their own soap operas, inventing a range of characters, settings (rooms, houses, neighbourhoods) and incidents in which the dramas and language unfold. Characters and their behaviour can be exaggerated: indeed there is much to be said for exaggerating the characters so that there is no illusion that these are real people and the students can feel free to be as inventive as they like and make as much use as possible of the language they have acquired.

Pictures have a central role to play in representing the characters, settings and incidents. Since it is an advantage to have exaggerated characters, a set of drawn caricatures provide a good starting point. These portraits can be drawn on a wall picture and can act as a constant reference point. The class can be asked to agree on the name, age, family status, interests, etc. for each of the characters.

The neighbourhood can be represented on a wall picture map as well. Streets, buildings, parks and so on can be located and named.

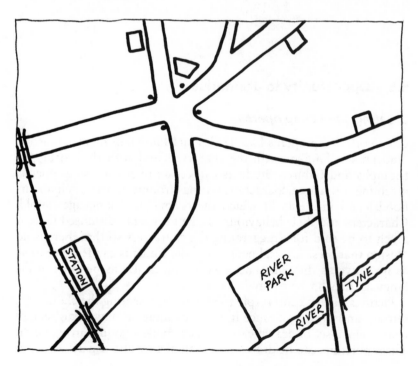

Soap opera can be the main vehicle of the lesson, or a 'one off' experience, or provide a ready and convenient reference for the teacher whenever she or he wants to give an example of language, or give a stimulus and guidance for dialogue work or story writing.

Here are a few examples of language activities which can arise: describing characters and places; saying what could or might happen; using 'if' and the conditionals; saying what has happened, is happening and will happen; putting forward ideas and arguing for them; working out dialogues; writing letters (for example, of complaint from one of the characters to a newspaper, or students writing to each other as if they were different characters in the soap opera); writing advertisements and newspaper articles; answering psychological tests on behalf of the character; role playing the characters in interviews; planning a week's holiday for one of the characters based on tourist information; describing a lost object; describing misunderstandings, an accident (what happens, discussion, role play, reports, letters), a celebration (planning and actually doing it in class as the characters), the town (history, socioeconomic character, leisure facilities); diaries of different characters, etc.

This brief list of ideas gives some indication of the potential of a soap opera running continually throughout the year, sometimes being the main vehicle of language learning, and sometimes only being referred to in passing. Although soap opera provides an opportunity for gross exaggeration, the topics and the language arising remain closely linked to the events of everyday life which most learners are preparing to deal with in the foreign language.

6 Mini-dialogues

Mini-dialogues are a long-established means of practising the speaking skill. They usually involve no more than two or three exchanges and they make use of sentence patterns given by the teacher. In this sense mini-dialogues give controlled or guided practice in the use of sentence patterns, in grammatical points, in the use of certain functions and in specific areas of vocabulary. Some of the examples which follow give an opportunity for the students to use all the language they know.

Mini-dialogues are communicative if there is some element of choice for the student in what he or she says. Even in the first very simple 'controlled' activity below the student can tell the truth about his or her likes and dislikes. Although the framework is artificial and imposed by the teacher, students often manage to say things about themselves which are true and to use their limited range of language to communicate interesting or amusing ideas.

6.1 Pictures and mini-dialogues

Pictures have an important role: they cue answers to questions or substitutions within sentence patterns and they provide a context for the language used. Pictures can be: a collection of pictures about the size of a postcard; a number of pictures on a single sheet of paper; a wall picture with a lot of details; drawings on the board or OHP; board games.

DRAWINGS OR PHOTOGRAPHS ON A THEME

116

Ideas for storing pictures for mini-dialogues are given on page 213.

6.2 Organising mini-dialogues

In most cases the teacher begins by demonstrating the mini-dialogue and the role of the pictures. It is essential that the students are confident in using the language and know what they have to do before they start to work in groups or pairs. This type of activity is for practice and not intended for the presentation of new language. If the teacher decides to provide a written model of the dialogue it can be written on the board or on an overhead transparency. Another way is to give each group an instruction card.

PICTURES: HOBBIES
HOW TO PLAY: Place the pictures in a pile upside down. Take it in turns to pick up a picture and to ask someone else a question.
STUDENT A: (picking up a picture of someone playing chess) Do you like playing chess?
STUDENT B: (telling the truth) Yes/No/Not very much/ Occasionally.

OPTIONAL LANGUAGE
It's great./It's very interesting./It's good fun./ It's very enjoyable./
It's boring./It's too difficult.

This type of activity has enormous potential for the language teacher. The coursebook being followed by the students will provide a source for dialogues as will J. Y. K. Kerr, *Picture Cue Cards for Oral Language Practice.*

6.3   Examples of mini-dialogues with pictures

203 *Do you like chess?*

Pictures required: Hobbies.
How to play: The pictures are placed in a pile upside down. The students take it in turns to pick up a picture and ask a question.
Student A: (*picking up a picture of someone playing chess*) Do you like playing chess?
Student B: (*telling the truth*) Yes / No / Not very much / Occasionally.
Optional language: It's great. / It's very interesting. / It's good fun. / It's very enjoyable. / It's boring. / It's too difficult.

118

204 *Travelling*

Pictures required: Places and transport.

How to play: The pictures are placed in two piles upside down. Student A picks up a picture in order to ask a question. Student B picks up a picture in order to answer.

Student A: *(picking up a picture of a place)* How did you go to the shops?

Student B: *(picking up a picture of a bus)* I went by bus.

Optional language: Yes, that's the best way. / That's crazy.

205 Variation

There is an opportunity for some amusement when the means of transport is ridiculous, for example, an elephant. The dialogue can be extended into open, free practice, either by student A saying, 'That's ridiculous!' or by student A asking a question and student B having to answer.

Student A: Why did you go by elephant?

Student B: Because I knew I would have a lot of shopping.

206 *Liking food*

Pictures required: Food.

How to play: The pictures are placed in a pile upside down. Students take it in turns to pick up a picture and then make a truthful statement about it, 'I like/don't like/sometimes like (plums)'. Each student must then repeat what the others have said. In this sense the activity becomes a 'Challenge to memorise'.

Student A: *(picking up a picture and putting it down in front of him or her, picture side up)* I like plums.

Student B: *(picking up a picture and putting it down in front of him or her)* I like bananas, and A likes plums.

Student C: *(picking up a picture and putting it down in front of him or her)* I don't like apples, B likes bananas and A likes plums.

E

207 *What would you do?*

Pictures required: Objects.

How to play: The pictures are placed in a pile upside down. One student picks up a picture and asks another what he or she would do with it on a desert island.

Student A: (*picking up a picture of a television*) What would you do with this television on a desert island?

Student B: I'd empty it and then keep fish in it.

208 *Inventions*

Pictures required: Modern inventions.

How to play: The pictures are placed upside down in a pile. Students take it in turns to pick up a picture and ask what William the Conqueror (any historical figure known to the students) would have done with it.

Student A: (*picking up a picture of a telephone*) If William the Conqueror had had this telephone what would he have done with it?

Student B: He'd have phoned up his wife and he'd have said, 'We've won!'

209 *Famous people*

Pictures required: Famous people.

How to play: The pictures are placed in a pile upside down. Students take it in turns to pick up a picture and then ask each other who the people are.

Student A: (*picking up a picture*) Who's this?

Student B: It's (Charlie Chaplin). / I don't know. / I'm not sure. / I think it's (Charlie Chaplin).

210 Variation

Student A: (*picking up a picture*) Isn't that Jane Fonda?

Student B: No, it isn't. It's (Meryl Streep).

Optional language: She's/He's marvellous/great/funny/horrible/useless.

211 *Can you tell me?*

Pictures required: Places (shops, institutions, etc.).

How to play: The pictures are placed upside down in a pile. Students take it in turns to take a picture and ask a question. The student replying gives directions which are correct for the area of the school or college.

Student A: *(picking up a picture of a post office)* Can you tell me how to get to a post office, please?

Student B: *(Answers as from the school; other students in the group agree or disagree.)*

Student A: *(Tries to repeat back to B the directions.)*

Optional language: I don't know this town. / I've got to post a letter. / You are lucky, there is one near here. / You are unlucky, I'm afraid. It's a long way from here.

212 *What is it?*

Pictures required: Objects.

How to play: The pictures are placed in a pile upside down. The first student takes the top eight pictures and lays them down, picture side up, on the table. The student then thinks of one of the pictures and the other students take it in turns to ask a question in order to find out which picture he or she is thinking about, for example, 'Is the object blue?' Direct questions, for example, 'Which picture are you thinking about?' or 'Are you thinking about the football?' are not allowed.

213 *Yesterday*

Pictures required: Actions and people (there should be about 40 pictures and there must be quite a few showing the same action).

How to play: The pictures are placed upside down in four piles (three piles of actions and one pile of people). The first student takes a picture of a person and asks a question. The second student takes two pictures of actions and makes a statement and then the third student takes another picture of an action and agrees with or contradicts the first student's statement.

Student A: *(taking a picture of a person and showing it to B)* What did Joan do yesterday?

Student B: *(picking up two pictures of actions)* She either went swimming or she played football.

Student C: *(picking up another action)* She played football. / She didn't do either. She went shopping.

Student A: Who did she go with?

Student D: *(picking up another picture of a person)* She went with a film actor.

FOUR PILES OF PICTURES UPSIDE DOWN

ONE PILE OF PEOPLE

THREE PILES OF ACTIONS

PICTURES PICKED UP BY THE FOUR STUDENTS A,B,C,D

Optional language: I'm not sure. / I think . . . / No, of course, she didn't! / That's nice. / The cheeky thing.

214 *What's it for?*

Pictures required: Objects and people.

How to play: The pictures are placed in two piles upside down. The first student picks up a picture from the 'object' pile. The second picks up a picture from the 'person' file.

Student A: (*picking up a picture from the object pile*) Whose is this?

Student B: (*picking up a picture from the person pile*) It's this girl's.

Student A: What does she use it for?

Student B: (*thinking fast!*) She keeps nuts in it.

215 *Connections*

Pictures required: Objects, people, places, transport and animals.

How to play: The pictures are placed upside down in five piles. The students take it in turns to take a picture from each pile, place the pictures on the table, and then make a statement which connects all five pictures. When the student has made a statement which the others find acceptable (realistic, amusing, outrageous) the pictures are put back into the piles.

216 *Game board*

Pictures required: Jobs.

How to play: A game board is required for this activity. The 'board' is simply a single sheet of paper with about twenty pictures on it. In the example given here the pictures represent professions. The students take it in turns to throw a die and then to proceed along the squares. When they land on a picture they have to say whether or not they would like to have that job and why.

Student A: (*landing on a picture of a miner*) I wouldn't like to be a miner because it's too dangerous.

Student B: (*landing on a picture of a teacher*) I would like to be a teacher because I would like to work with lovely students like us!

Note It is worth noting that the basic layout of many games boards is similar: a 'road' of connected squares, which can be made easily.

TWO BASIC
DESIGNS OF
BOARD GAME

Players throw the die
and then move
along the squares.

When they land on a
square players
must respond to
the text or picture
which is there.

If they land on a
CHANCE square
they must take
a card and follow
the instructions.

Pictures and/or texts can be placed on each square and changed each time a new game is needed.

7 Role play and simulation

In **role play** the students imagine they are in a specified situation. They may take on the character and role of someone else or be themselves. Pictures can be used to illustrate: the context of the situation (a restaurant); the people involved (a customer and a waiter); the subject of the communication ('There is no fish but there is beef').

The way in which the teacher introduces and helps to make these activities successful is not described in detail below. In general, for role play to be successful the students must know what they have to do and have the language to do it with. If they are not familiar with an activity then it would be advisable for the teacher to act it out with the class first. In the first activity below, the teacher could play the part of the shop assistant and ask four students to come to the front of the class to be the customers. The teacher can decide how far the role play should be controlled in terms of the sentence patterns used and how far it should be guided by a model which the students can all see. The teacher might also find it useful to write on the board any important phrases or words which the students will need.

Shopping

217 Groupwork. One student in the group is given a wide selection of pictures of objects which could all be bought in a general store. Each of the others is given a shopping list. The students take it in turns to ask for one of their items. The 'shop assistant' gives it to them if he or she has it. At beginner level the students can simply name the item they want. At a higher level the students might have to specify the sort of object and its price.

218 **Variation** The shop assistant deliberately gives the customer the wrong object. The customer must protest and correct the assistant.
Customer: Not the green one, the red one.

219 **Variation** Classwork. Five or six shop assistants are appointed and place themselves with their goods (pictures) somewhere in the classroom. For each object they are selling they must also have a price. All the other students have shopping lists (these can be written earlier in

the lesson). Each student also has a limited amount of money to spend. The students must then find the shopkeepers who have their goods and make sure that the price is right. The customer is successful if he or she can return home having bought everything on his or her shopping list with the amount of money allowed.

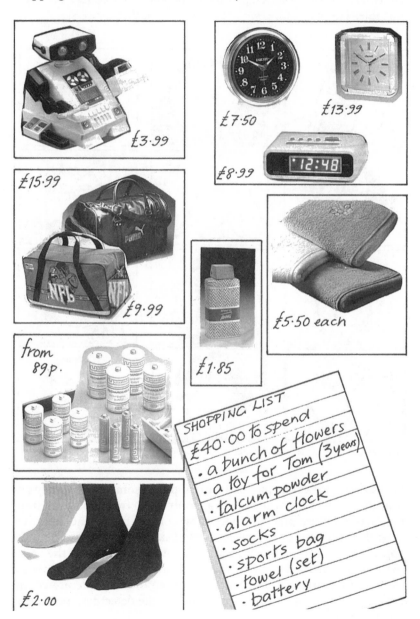

SHOPPING LIST
£40·00 to spend
· a bunch of flowers
· a toy for Tom (3 years)
· talcum powder
· alarm clock
· socks
· sports bag
· towel (set)
· battery

Detectives

220 Groupwork. There should be five students in the group. Two of the
students are detectives and they should each get one picture of a different suspect (a man or a woman). Each of the other students is a
witness. A pile of about ten pictures of people is placed face down on
the table. There must be two copies of each of the suspects.

TWO CARDS FOR THE DETECTIVES. TEN CARDS FOR THE WITNESSES.

Each witness takes one picture from the pile of someone that they saw
near the scene of the crime. They are only given two minutes to study
the picture before placing it face down on the table. The detectives
keep their pictures of the suspects and ask questions to find out the
appearance of the people the witnesses saw. The aim is for the detectives to find their suspects. If they are sure that the witness saw the
suspect, they arrest the suspect by turning over the picture on the
table. If it is the same picture as the one in the detective's possession
the detective keeps it.

Dramatic dialogues

21 Pairwork. A number of pictures are displayed for all the class to see. The pictures should have people in them, preferably appearing to be speaking to each other. (Pictures with a sense of drama will normally produce the liveliest results.) In pairs, students look at all the pictures and then decide on one of them. They study the people and try to imagine their concerns. The students write a dialogue and then act it out for the class. The class decides which picture the pair were representing.

Picture drama

22 Groupwork. A picture is displayed so that the whole class can see it. Each group studies the picture and then creates a five minute drama which finishes with the picture. The students can either make notes or write out the dialogue in full. The other groups watch the drama, and because the same picture is referred to, their interest is retained.

Person, scene and object

23 Groupwork. Each student is given a picture of a person, and each group is given a picture of a scene and a picture of an object. The students study their individual pictures and adopt the character of that person. The group then works out a drama based on the scene, the object and their characters, which they then act out.

Picture sequence

224 Pairwork and groupwork. Each pair is given a picture sequence (including people) without a text. They study the pictures and then work out a dialogue to go with them. Pairs take it in turns to act out their dialogues for each other.

Magazine mask

225 Pairwork or groupwork. Each student is given a large magazine photograph of someone's face. The students work out a character for their face. In pairs or small groups they evolve and act out a dialogue holding the photograph in front of their face.

The party

226 Classwork. This role play can be done at various levels determined by the number and type of pictures given to the students. At a simple level each student is given a picture of an occupation which he or she adopts in the role play. The student might also be given two or three pictures of hobbies and sports. The aim of the role play is for students to look for other people at a party with the same interests and/or jobs. If more pictures are given to the students, clearly the conversations can be extended. After the role play students can write to the new acquaintance they met at the party.

Note It is advisable to include a number of similar pictures.

27 **Variation** A mystery picture is also given (it might be something to be proud of or a disgrace). Through conversation each student must try to find out what it is.

(Adapted from Charles Lockhart and Mary Woodiwiss, 'More activities with small cards'.)

Interviewing the famous

28 Pairwork. One student is the interviewer and the other is a famous person. The famous person is given a number of pictures of people, places and events, and must decide how each picture relates to his or her life. The interviewer is responsible for asking the questions and making sure every picture is accounted for.

(Adapted from Charles Lockhart and Mary Woodiwiss, 'More activities with small cards'.)

Picture strip sequence play

29 Groupwork. Each group invents a picture strip sequence of a dramatic incident; they draw it out and can add speech bubbles if they wish. The number of main characters should equal the number of students in the group. When the strip has been drawn, the students each take a role from the story which they dramatise and rehearse. When they are ready they give their strip to another group to look at for a few minutes before acting out the play for them.

Finally, each student writes up a report or a story from his or her own point of view in the play. They then take it in turns to read their reports or stories to each other.

Inventing a character

30 Pairwork and groupwork (about eight to ten students). At first the students work in pairs, and each student tells his or her partner what sort of person to draw. (The drawings do not need to be good but they should be characterful. It is helpful if they are at least 10 to 12 centimetres high. The drawing should be placed at the top of an A4 sheet of paper.) When the drawing is done the first pair gives the person a name and age, writing them down beneath the drawing. They then pass it on to the next pair of students who write down the person's job and his or her main interests in life. The next pair writes down his or her worst characteristic and the next pair his or her best characteristic. The paper can be folded into strips so that the students are not able to see the previous information, just the figure, name and age.

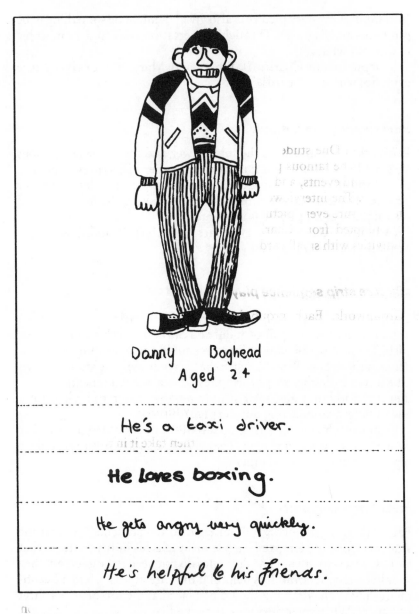

Danny Boghead
Aged 24

He's a taxi driver.

He loves boxing.

He gets angry very quickly.

He's helpful to his friends.

After the drawings and descriptive sentences have been completed each student adopts one of the characters as his or her own. In groups they then imagine that they have met in a railway station just after their train has been cancelled.

(Adapted from Lou Spaventa (ed.), *Towards the Creative Teaching of English*.)

Simlations are an extension of role play: the students take on the character of someone else and a problem is given which the various characters must try to solve. Simulations are rather more complicated than role plays and take more time to carry out. The advantage of a well-organised simulation is the immense enthusiasm and commitment which it generates. Pictures have a role to play in some simulations by providing a context and non-verbal information which might, for example, illustrate the problem to be solved or ways of solving the problem.

The examples that follow are brief outlines and are not intended to be exhaustive descriptions of simulations. Teachers would need to adapt and expand the ideas to suit their situation and their students' needs.

Holiday

231 Groupwork and classwork. There are two stages in the preparation for this simulation: making picture displays and devising checklists, both done by the students.

Each group is asked to make a display of pictures which comprehensively represent a holiday location; for example, sea and sunbathing, walking, touring, culture. The pictures, maps, costs, etc. can be taken from holiday brochures and should be mounted on large sheets of paper which are suitable for wall displays.

The students, in groups or as a class, draw up a checklist of the factors to be taken into account when planning a holiday. The final product should include cost, length of time, time of year, touring or staying in one place, the importance of the sea and beaches for sunbathing, water sports, other sports, cultural interests, culinary interests, etc. If the students are working in groups they can pool their ideas to draw up a class list.

The simulation: each student is given a picture of a person which provides the starting point for their role. Each student examines their picture and tries to imagine what sort of person they might be, their interests, concerns and personality. If they wish to they can make brief notes of their ideas.

The students then consider their role in relation to the type of holiday that person would like. The checklist will provide prompts for things to consider. The students then set off around the class to find at least one other student, with similar needs, to plan a holiday with. They form new pairs or groups and, using the information on the wallcharts, plan the details of their holiday.

Each pair or group then tells the class which of the holidays they have chosen and how it fits in with the different needs of the people in the group.

Buying paintings

232 Groupwork and classwork. A number of reproductions of paintings are displayed.

Each group of students is told that it is a 'buying committee' on behalf of: a nurses' room in a hospital; a patients' ward in a hospital; a waiting room in a hospital; a hall in a school; a staff room in a school; and a classroom in a school. A complication can be added if each buying committee is allocated a limited amount of money and the pictures are given prices. A further complication can be added if the committee is told that it does not have to give pictures to all the places on its list but can decide on priorities.

Each student is given a description of a character which he or she must adopt. When the committee begins to discuss which pictures to buy each student must argue as if he or she is the character given to them.

At the end of the activity, new groups of students are formed with one representative from each of the buying committees. Each student then reports on his or her committee's plan and different policies are discussed.

HOSPITAL WAITING ROOM
....
The Council has decided to buy a picture for the hospital's
new waiting room. The suggestion is that the Council buy
reproductions of famous paintings.

You are an art teacher and you think this is an opportunity to
educate people. You think the picture should be a reproduction of
one of the greatest paintings ever painted.
....

HOSPITAL WAITING ROOM
....
The Council has decided to buy a picture for the hospital's
new waiting room. The suggestion is that the Council buy
reproductions of famous paintings.

You are a local business man and you can supply the Council with a
reproduction and in a frame ready to put on the wall. You are
willing to sell the reproduction to the Council at a cheap rate.
You have got a lot of pictures of gypsy girls and of green waves
to sell.
....

HOSPITAL WAITING ROOM
....
The Council has decided to buy a picture for the hospital's
new waiting room. The suggestion is that the Council buy
reproductions of famous paintings.

You are the Head of the local Art School.
You are strongly against buying reproductions. The city
should support living artists and buy an original painting
from a resident artist or a student.

You think it should be bright, colourful and cheer people up.
....

HOSPITAL WAITING ROOM
....
The Council has decided to buy a picture for the hospital's
new waiting room. The suggestion is that the Council buy
reproductions of famous paintings.

You are the President of the local Water Colour Society. You and
your society paint landscapes in a traditional way. You think it
is obvious that people would like a lovely picture of the country
to forget about their problems. You do not agree with 'modern
art'. You do not mind if it is a reproduction or not.
....

Pictures have a major role to play in the development of student skills in listening and reading. There are two reasons in particular for this:

1. The meanings we derive from words are affected by the context they are in: pictures can represent or contribute much to the creation of contexts in the the classroom.
2. It is often helpful if the students can respond to a text non-verbally: pictures provide an opportunity for non-verbal response.

8   Pictures and the teaching of meaning

Pictures have been used for centuries to help students understand various aspects of foreign languages. The pictures have motivated the students, made the subjects they are dealing with clearer, and illustrated the general idea and forms of an object or action which are particular to a culture. The general idea of 'house' can be translated verbally, but not the physical structure of 'house' as found in different countries and even areas of countries.

136

Pictures have a role to play in the teaching of meaning even in traditional grammar translation methods. In recent years, teachers have given more emphasis to the importance of introducing new language to students within appropriate contexts. Superficially, this approach might seem more laborious than teaching meaning by translation. However, a central aim of the teacher is to help the students develop skill and confidence in searching for meaning themselves. Translation might often provide meaning quickly but it does not develop this essential learning strategy which the students can continue to draw on long after they have left the classroom.

Contexts, pictures and meanings

It is now generally accepted in language teaching that we must learn to deal with chunks of language above the level of the word or the sentence. When we try to understand someone speaking we normally take into account not only their verbal language but their appearance, the sound of their voice, their behaviour, their relationship to others, the situation and the setting. If we are reading we are affected to some extent by the appearance of the book or newspaper or greetings card. The non-verbal information helps us to predict what the text might be about, and this ability to predict helps us to recognise meaning more quickly than if we had to sort it out solely from what we hear or read.

Pictures can represent these non-verbal sources of information. Indeed, they and what they represent are centrally bound up with the nature of communication itself. What we see affects how we interpret what we hear and vice versa. How someone is dressed, how they behave and what they say are inextricably linked in our minds.

Communicative methodology emphasises the need for teachers to prepare students to communicate making use of non-verbal as well as verbal means. The teacher has the task of creating a context within which communication that takes into account both verbal and non-verbal factors can take place.

Creating contexts

What is context? We can analyse it in this way:

Context: setting (place, objects)
participants (appearance, actions, relations with others)
purpose (what the people are trying to achieve)
topic (the subject of the communication)
channel (words heard or read, their tone or appearance)

The art of the teacher is to create contexts in which the students' minds are focussed on the meaning and use of the language being taught and the language is experienced by the students as essential to their participation in the activity. The language must be intrinsic to the context, not forced or artificial; a native speaker should feel at ease using the same language for the same purpose.

Let us take an example: *The Guinness Book of Records*. Superlative and comparative facts are intrinsic to *The Guinness Book of Records*; it would be impossible to talk about records if we couldn't make use of these forms.

This example provides us with two other important points. First, the context for the introduction of 'new' language should interest the students. *The Guinness Book of Records* is a very popular book, with enormous sales, so it has a good chance of being of interest. Secondly, the context chosen should involve the students so that they can try to make their own use of the new language forms. Students can talk about records they know about or about their own personal records. Students could even do things to create records in the classroom, like making and flying paper planes and seeing whose plane goes the furthest, listing as many words as possible beginning with the same letter, talking without hesitation for as long as possible, naming as many things as possible within a picture.

8.1 Establishing meaning

Introducing meaning is only the first step in a long process in which students become familiar with an aspect of language and what it represents. The students must be given an opportunity both to experience and use the language in a variety of contexts if it is to become a significant part of their language resource. This chapter is concerned with the initial focussing on meaning and the following chapters with the extension of the students' familiarity with meaning, form and use necessary for effective communication.

Our natural inclination is to search for meaning and this is an essential aspect of language learning and development. In foreign language learning there is rarely enough time for this searching to be allowed to happen in a random way. The teacher is responsible for introducing 'new' language at a considerable pace. The use of suitable pictures in the introduction of language can speed the process by which students assimilate meaning.

The remaining part of this chapter describes and to some extent assesses the appropriacy of a number of ways of using pictures in the introduction of language which is new to the students.

8.2 Bringing the outside world into the classroom

This section is concerned with the role of pictures in the teaching of meaning. The limitations of most classrooms mean that the outside world must be simulated. If the representation and reference to the outside world are understood by the students in the way intended, then it is hoped they will understand the 'new' language associated with them. The basis of all the activities involves the teacher, tape or written text describing the content of a picture, with the picture illustrating the meaning of the 'new' language. Alternatively, one or more pictures might illustrate a dialogue or story; if the dialogue and pictures are understood then it is hoped that the language which is new to the student will also be understood. The activities in this section, although of value if used appropriately, would not be done by the teacher and students unless they were learning a foreign language. These activities thus contrast with those in section 8.3 which concern events in the classroom which are of more authentic interest.

Using one example

233 Elephant

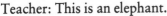

Teacher: This is an elephant.

There are many things which are difficult to bring into the classroom, including elephants! Pictures make it possible. However, a single example of an object is sometimes insufficient to focus the students' minds on the interpretation the teacher wishes to convey. In the example of the elephant we do not necessarily want to name the animal. The language aim could be to say how big it is.

Using several examples

In order to focus the students' minds on one aspect of a picture it is sometimes helpful to show several pictures which all have one key point in common.

234 He is horrified

The first picture below seen by itself could illustrate, 'He has seen a ghost'. Together with the other pictures it is more likely to be seen as, 'He is horrified' in that it is applicable to all three situations.

235 Working

Teacher: He's cooking. She's driving. He's digging. She's telephoning. They are working.

Sometimes it is necessary to show instances of a collective idea, in this case to introduce the verb 'work'.

Comparing examples

Comparing two similar objects, actions or concepts can focus the students' minds on the difference between them.

236 Running and sprinting

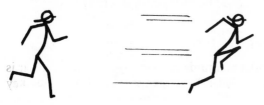

Teacher: She's running and she's sprinting.

237 Say and tell

After introducing these words in a broader context, the pictures below may help students to distinguish their usage.

Teacher: He says he likes apples.

He tells Wendy he likes apples.

238 Sounds

Sounds and the words containing them can be illustrated on cards, used for presenting and then for practice.

239 Formality / informality 1

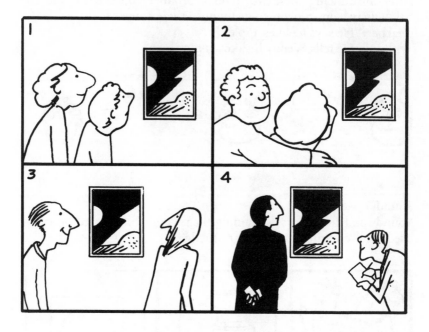

Teacher or tape: (*Picture 1*) Do you like it?
(*Picture 2*) Like it?
(*Picture 3*) May I ask you if you like it?
(*Picture 4*) Excuse me, please. Would you mind if I
ask you whether you like the picture?

240 Formality / informality 2

Teacher or tape: (*Picture 1*) How do you do.
(*Picture 2*) Hi!
(*Picture 3*) Hello!

41 Stress

Teacher or tape: (*Picture 1*) I'm going there!
(*Picture 2*) I'm going there!

Contrasting examples

Contrast can be used to focus the students' minds on two contrasting concepts rather than on other features which the pictures are illustrating.

242 Likes and dislikes

Teacher: He likes sweets. She doesn't like sweets.
The two sides of a piece of card are used for these two pictures. The contrast helps to teach the meaning of each one.

243 Animals
If a number of animals are shown and the pattern of the sentence remains unchanged it is likely that the speaker is naming the animals.

Teacher: This is an elephant. This is a tiger. This is a giraffe, etc.

Whole and parts

244 Parts of a tree

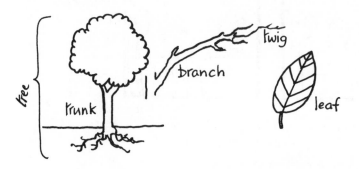

The meanings of the words naming the parts of a tree are made apparent by seeing the tree as a whole. The meaning of the word 'tree' is made clear by seeing the parts assembled into the whole.

245 Family tree

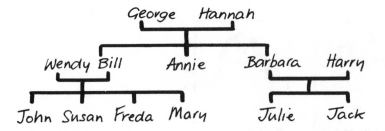

This diagram is a family tree. It offers a similar way of contextualising meaning to 'tree' as in the example above. In this case, it is a 'belonging' relationship rather than a physical component relationship.

246 Sentence building

Pictures can be used together with words to demonstrate word order and relationships.

Diagrammatic pictures

47 Prepositions

The addition of symbols to pictures can focus the students' attention on the concepts which the teacher has in mind.

Sequence

Some concepts are intrinsically bound up with a sequence of events. In the example below the blank panel would have no meaning unless we had seen the first two panels.

48 Present perfect

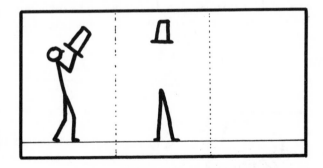

Teacher: He's going to make himself invisible. He's making himself invisible. He's made himself invisible.

The sequence of pictures contextualises, however briefly, these three tense forms. If the drawings are made on a piece of folded paper the story can be told with a little more drama as the teacher reveals the actions one by one. Meaning is highlighted in this example partly by the sequence of events and partly by the contrast. (For more examples of the use of folding paper, see page 26.)

249 Run back

Teacher: He left home and he went for a walk. Then a dark cloud
came and it began to rain. So he ran back home.
The idea of running back is only to be understood if one knows where
he has come from!

Note 1 The traditional way of using a sequence of pictures is as
follows:
1. The students look at the pictures and guess at the story line.
2. The students listen to the recording (or the teacher).
3. The teacher asks questions which focus on the meaning of the
story and on the 'new' language forms.
4. The students act out the dialogue or they retell the story.
5. Various written and oral exercises are done by the students.

Note 2 The teacher's or the students' own drawings can be done on
the board or on a large sheet of paper to illustrate the sequence.

Cause and effect

250 Because

Teacher: He caught a cold because he got wet.
The meaning of 'because' in this example can only be conveyed by
showing cause and effect.

51 Can / because

Teacher: Can he see the girl?
Student: No.
Teacher: Why not?
Student: Because the tree is in the way.

52 Would / if

Teacher: What would happen if she stood up?
Student: She would hit her head on the ceiling.

8.3 Contributing to the world of the classroom

In this way of using pictures the teacher and students create an event in the classroom. The activities described have intrinsic interest of their own: they do not depend on outside and potential usefulness. The teacher and students are doing things which they might well do in their own language. They are exploring, expressing, playing and using language as a natural part of these activities. The picture is a part of the event and the event as a whole highlights the meaning of the 'new' language.

147

253 What's this?

Teacher: (*drawing the above on the board*) What's this?
Student: It's a table.

The drawing is puzzling, so the question 'What's this?' is authentic. If the teacher points at a table (or an obvious picture of one) and says, 'What's this?' he or she is really saying, 'What's the word for this in English?'

254 Comparing graphs

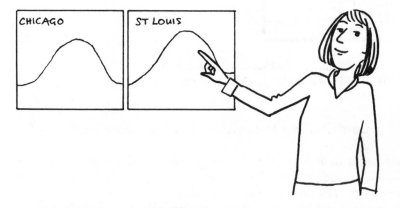

Teacher: (*pointing at the two graphs*) It's very hot in the summer in Chicago, but it's hotter in St Louis.

Graphs and charts often invite comparisons and hence the language to express them.

148

55 Comparing lines

Teacher: (*gesturing to contrast longest and shortest and pointing at the lines*) Which is the longest line? I think it's the yellow one. Which is the longest line? Do you think the yellow line is the longest? (*the teacher continues to use 'the longest' in various ways and then writes a simple statement on the board, 'The yellow line is the longest.'*)

This activity naturally challenges the students to express their view.

56 What does this mean?

Teacher: (*pointing to a sign*) This means danger. (*showing another sign*) What does this mean? That means danger as well.

An extended study of the design and interpretation of signs provides a considerable opportunity for the use of 'to mean' and the vocabulary associated with the subject of the signs.

257 Like and prefer

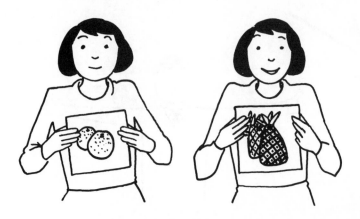

Teacher: (*picking up a picture of some oranges and looking pleased*)
I like oranges! (*picking up a picture of some pineapples and
demonstrating preference, for example, putting down the
oranges*) But I prefer pineapples!

The teacher repeats the process with a number of different examples,
gradually inviting the students to express their feelings.

258 Going to / will

Teacher: (*ready to draw on the board*) I'm going to draw a house.
First of all, I'll draw the walls. (*draws a rectangle*) Then I'll
draw the door. (*draws a small rectangle for the door*)

The teacher can continue in this way, continually contextualising the
future tense form.

150

259 I can't see it. Can you?

Teacher: (*holding up a picture which is far too small for the students to see*) What's this? (*students can't see it*) What's wrong? Can't you see it? (*gives a student the picture to hold up at the front of the class and goes to the back of the class him or herself*) Oh no, I can't see it. Can you see it? Come a little closer. No, I can't see it. Can you see it? Can you? Oh! I can see it!

260 What could you do with it?

The teacher shows various pictures of simple objects and asks the students what they could do with them. At first the teacher suggests the ideas and in this way introduces the language form.

Teacher: (*showing a picture of a brick*) What could I do with this brick? Er . . . I could put it on the floor by the cupboard and then I could stand on it and then I could reach the top of the cupboard. Or I could put it on top of my papers to stop them falling off the desk.

F

261 If I had ... I would ...

The teacher needs several catalogues or advertisements, for example, for household goods, foods, cars, clothes, holidays. Other ways of spending money might also be included, for example, information on charity organisations like Oxfam.

Teacher: (*looking at a holiday catalogue*) Where would I like to go for my holidays? If I had lots of money I think I would like to go to Australia. I would be able to see the koala bears. What else would I be able to do? Oh yes, I would be able to visit the Great Barrier Reef. (*showing pictures of these places*)

262 I should have ...

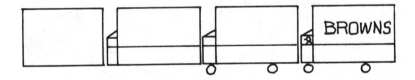

Teacher: (*draws a rectangle*) What's this?
Student A: A door?
Teacher: No, it's a lorry. I should have drawn some wheels. (*draws them*) And I should have drawn a cab at the front. (*draws it*) Then you would have recognised it. I could have drawn a name on the lorry (*draws it on*) but it wouldn't have helped you very much.

If this idea is repeated with different examples, 'should have', 'would have' and 'could have' will begin to have their areas of meaning defined in the students' minds.

63 **What might happen?**

The teacher encourages the students to propose various developments in a story based on the picture. The activity then involves inventing with 'might' and telling the story in the past tense. Initially, the teacher suggests what might happen and then the students become involved using the same pattern.

Teacher: What might happen next? The cat might bite the baby. Do you think so? OK. So the family was sitting in the room. Father was reading and mother was sleeping. Suddenly the cat bit the baby!

What might happen next? The baby might cry. Do you think so? OK. The cat bit the baby and then the baby cried. And what do you think might happen then?

Student: The mother might beat the baby.

Teacher: So the mother beat the baby! And then what might happen?

Student: The mother might throw the baby through the window.

264 What might be happening?

The teacher draws an ambiguous picture and then asks what is happening. The teacher speculates and demonstrates how to say what might be happening.

Teacher: He's running. And he's looking behind him. Somebody might be chasing him. He may have stolen something. Or he could be running in a race and looking to see if someone is near him.

There is another man. He's lying down. He might be dead. The first man might have killed him. Or he might be sleeping. But if he's sleeping the other man wouldn't run away. He might do though, because he might have stolen the second man's money.

The woman is holding a gun. She must have shot the second man. And the first man might be running away because he is frightened. Or she . . .

The teacher gradually encourages the students to make their own suggestions. Finally, the teacher and the students try to summarise the story. Following the classwork, students work with their neighbour and devise another modal story which they then try out on at least one other pair.

265 **A bridge was built**

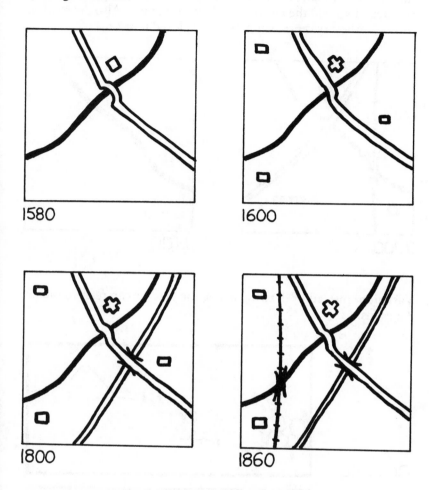

Describing the growth of a town offers a natural context for the use of various tenses in the passive. The teacher draws a map of a district as it was in the past on the board. (It could be an invented place or a map of the students' home area.) The teacher writes a date next to the map and, using appropriate past tense forms, describes what was there at that time. The teacher then changes the date and makes changes to the map.

Teacher: A bridge was built in 1580 and the forest was cut down. By 1600 three farms had been built and the church had been enlarged. The canal was dug between 1780 and 1800, and the railway was built in 1860.

155

Future reference can be made by adding predicted changes to the map.

Teacher: By 2000 the airport will have been built. Also the roads in
the city centre will have been closed to traffic.

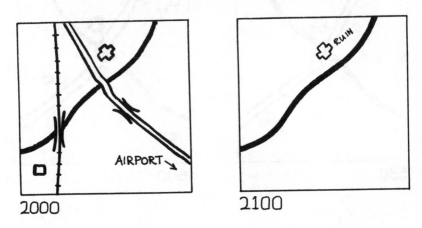

266 **Variation** Instead of drawing maps, the teacher can refer to picture
diagrams.

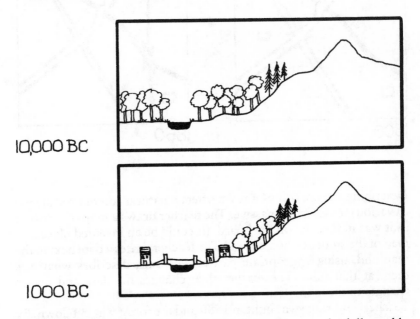

This introduction to various tenses in the passive can be followed by
the students talking about their own district and perhaps going on to
make their own maps or drawings of their district or a fantasy district.

156

267 Autobiography

The continuous past tense interrupted by the simple past is a common feature in descriptions of experiences. This relationship between the two tense forms is contextualised if the teacher tells the students about an event or set of events in his or her life. By sketching on the board at the same time as talking, the impression of storytelling, of a continuous action and of a sudden interruption can be dramatically conveyed. The new language is understood in the context of the story, the meaning of which is made clear by the pictures and known language.

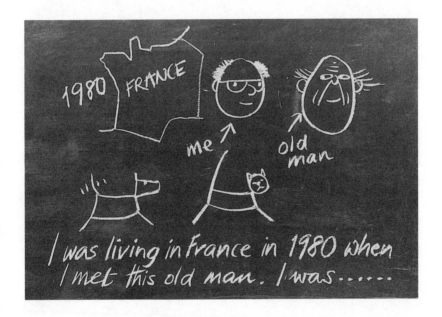

268 Past, present and future

The teacher draws a complicated picture on the board. While the picture is being built up the teacher asks the students to describe what is happening.

When the picture has been built up and described the teacher erases most of it. Very small bits of all the people are left, for example, a foot, a hand, a hat, and an eye. The teacher then challenges the students' memories. (It is essential to have drawn a really complicated picture or this is not a convincing challenge.) The teacher and students identify the parts of the people and then say what the people were doing. Each tense used to describe the picture when it was visible on the board is now modified.

157

Picture on the board:
The woman has let the dog out.
The dog is chasing the cat.
The cat has bumped into the man.
The man has fallen against the ladder.
The postman has given the parcel to the man.
The man is going to give the parcel to the girl.

Trying to remember the picture:
The woman had let the dog out.
The dog was chasing the cat.
The cat had bumped into the man.
The man had fallen against the ladder.
The postman had given the parcel to the man.
The man was going to give the parcel to the girl.

9 Developing listening and reading skills

For many years reading in a foreign language classroom was limited primarily to translation work and listening to the foreign language was incidental to other classroom activities. In recent times methodology has changed to encourage the development of a wider range of receptive skills. This broadening of the scope of classroom practice has been reflected in the growing variety of teaching techniques employed. The use of pictures should be seen against this richer and more varied methodological background.

9.1 Types of skills

With listening and reading there are four easily identifiable skills:
- Skimming, which is listening or reading for gist, e.g. quickly glancing through an article to see if it interests us or 'half listening' to a radio programme so we can focus our full attention on an item if it interests us.
- Scanning, which is listening or reading to locate specific information, e.g. locating a telephone number in a directory or from a recorded message.
- Intensive listening or reading where the listener/ reader is trying to absorb all the information given, e.g. listening to or reading dosage instructions for medicine.
- Extensive listening and reading where the listener/reader deals with a longer text as a whole, which requires the ability to understand the component parts and their contribution to the overall meaning, e.g. reading a newspaper article, short story or novel or listening to a radio play.

With exercises designed to develop particular skills in listening and reading, pictures can be used to provide either the general context or to illustrate particular points. In addition, pictures can be used by the students to show their understanding non-verbally by, for example, pointing to a detail in a picture or adding information to a drawing.

159

9.2   Micro-skills

Predicting   In any situation we use our knowledge and understanding of the circumstances to make predictions about what we think will happen or be said. For example, when approached by a waitress on entering a restaurant we would expect her to greet us and ask something along the lines of, 'Table for how many?' 'Smoking or non-smoking?' 'Do you have a reservation?'

Non-verbal information gathered from the situation as a whole, our understanding of the relationship between the people involved and how they behave affects what we hear and how we interpret it. In the language classroom pictures can, to some extent, provide this type of non-verbal information and help students to predict the content of a text and to respond to the language appropriately.

Recognising implied meaning   As so much can be understood from the context in which something is said it is often unnecessary for a speaker to be totally explicit. For example, 'It's red' could express fear or anger if said by a passenger in a car speeding towards traffic lights or it could express pleasure or disappointment if said by someone opening a present. So, not only does context help us to make predictions, it also allows the speaker or writer to assume that the listener or reader will understand what is being referred to. Pictures are invaluable in helping the students to 'see' the setting the speakers are in as well as their appearance, behaviour and mood, and thus help the learners to understand the text and its implied meanings.

Traditionally, pictures have been used to add interest, to introduce cultural and contextual reference and to indicate the meaning of associated language. These established roles for pictures are still highly relevant in promoting the development of the wider range of listening and reading skills described above. Now these roles are more widely interpreted and are added to by the role of pictures in setting and directing tasks for the students to do.

9.3   Stages

Pre-listening and reading   Pre-listening or reading work should involve the student, create a sense of purpose in reading or listening and help to focus the student's mind on the content of the text. For example, before playing a tape recording of a news broadcast, headlines and/or photographs from the same day's newspaper can be looked at and the students can discuss what they think the news headlines or photographs refer to. Then, as they listen, the students can identify which of the headlines or photographs are covered in the broadcast. Pre-listening or reading work should prepare the student for the content of the text and give them a particular task to do.

During listening and reading Pictures can help the student to keep in mind the overall context, the nature and the behaviour of the pro- tagonists and the situation they are in. Pictures can be used to set the students a task to do while listening or reading. Tasks done while listening must be quick to do, otherwise the student may miss a lot of the text while doing the task. For example, students can check the sequence of some pictures and reorder them if necessary.

Post-listening and reading The task done while listening to or read- ing a text (or immediately afterwards) can help to show what the students have understood and how they have responded to it. The stu- dents' responses can provide the basis for discussion, objective analysis or the expression of a more personal reaction. For example, the students can compare their sequencing of a set of pictures before going on to a writing task. It can also lead to further work such as role playing or writing.

Pictures can have a central role in all three stages. They can represent the speakers, their appearance, their behaviour, the setting and the situation. This information can motivate the learner, and focus the learner's mind on the likely content and mood of the message. Pic- tures can, on the other hand, be a complement to the text so that neither is understandable without the other. A picture might add extra information which allows the learner to infer what is intended but not clearly stated in the text.

The descriptions of activities which follow do not suggest which of the three stages they might be used for because many of them can be adapted for use at any stage. But, as in Part B Emphasis on speaking and writing, the activities are categorised according to what cognitive challenge is involved.

10 Communication and challenges

10.1 Challenge to identify

In all the activities included under 'Challenge to identify' the students listen to or read a text and show their understanding of an aspect of it by identifying a picture or part of a picture.

Texts might be: descriptions, narrations, dialogues, poems, recipes, notes, advertisements, rules, etc. These texts might be about people: their appearance, thoughts, intentions, ambitions, fears, relationships; or about places or objects: their appearance, function, position in the picture; or about ideas.

Ways of identifying non-verbally might be: pointing, ticking, holding up, or drawing. Minimal verbal responses might be made by naming or repeating. In most of the activities below the reading or listening and the non-verbal or minimal verbal response are seen as part of a broader activity, sometimes involving all four skills.

Meet me at the airport

269 Classwork or groupwork. The students are shown a complicated picture (or a number of small pictures) including many people. They look at the people in the picture and discuss the similarities and differences between them. The students then listen to or read a description of someone who is going to meet them at the airport. Each student then indicates the one who they think has been described. Afterwards, these judgements are compared and the general idea of appearances can be discussed and personal experiences exchanged.

Note Clearly there are contexts other than airports in which people are described.

People and their thoughts

270 Groupwork. The students are shown a variety of pictures of people. They study them in groups and discuss what sort of people they might be and what sort of things might concern them. The students then listen to or read a text which describes what one of the people is think-

162

ing. The students then indicate which person they have identified as thinking the thoughts. Afterwards, the students could write a number of speech and thought bubbles of their own for the different people and see if other students can guess which people they had in mind.

Objects and their uses

271 Groupwork or individual work. The students look at a picture showing many objects and try to deduce what the objects are used for. The students listen to or read a text which describes what might be done with a particular object. They indicate which object has been referred to. Afterwards, the students can say how they decided upon their chosen object.

Incomplete picture

272 Individual work. The students are given an incomplete picture. They study the picture and speculate what might be missing and lightly sketch in the missing parts. They then listen to or read a text and draw in the missing parts of the picture. Afterwards, the students compare what they have done.

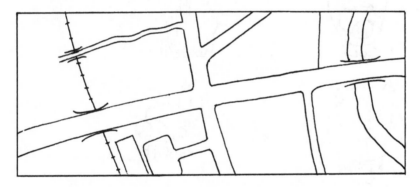

THE STUDENT DRAWS IN THE MISSING PARTS

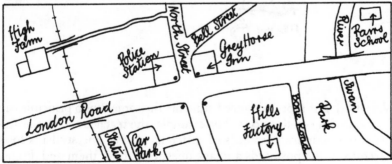

Bingo

Classwork. Bingo is a well-known game which presents a 'challenge to identify' to the students. It can be played with spoken and written text or with spoken text and pictures. Here are a few examples of the many versions of Bingo.

273 The teacher shows about twenty pictures of objects to the students. The students name the objects and the words are written on the board. Each student writes down any five of the words. The teacher then holds up the pictures in random order. The students cross off the names on their lists as the teacher holds up the picture of each. The first student to cross off all his or her names shouts 'Bingo!'

274 **Variation** The twenty words are collected on the board as above. The students make rapid sketches of five of the objects. The teacher can either name or describe the objects.

275 **Variation** For more advanced students the same Bingo principle can be used with equal success. For example, the teacher shows the students ten or more postcards of different places. The students look carefully at the postcards and ask questions about them and discuss

them. They should make notes describing five of the cards: what each card shows and where it is from.

Then the teacher describes the cards randomly and the students tick their descriptions when they hear the place being described. Clearly this can be done at very different conceptual and linguistic levels. For example, at a most demanding level the teacher might discuss the economic or historical associations of the place and not refer directly to what is in the picture. The students shout 'Bingo' when they think their five postcards have been referred to.

10.2 Challenge to match

In these activities the students are given a number of texts and pictures. Each text has to be matched with the most appropriate picture.

People and speech bubbles

It's going to rain.
Would you believe it?
We need some potatoes.

Have you seen the pen?
That's a good one!
And then she hit me!

176 Groupwork. The students are given various pictures of people talking, with empty speech bubbles. They first of all discuss what the people might be saying. Then they are given a number of sentences and decide which they think are the most likely ones to fit the picture. Once they have decided, they write them into the bubbles.

True or false

277 Groupwork or individual work. The students are given a picture together with several sentences about it. They must decide which of the sentences are true and which are false.

```
The young man is in a restaurant.
The restaurant is in the country.
His friend is telling him a joke.
He's thinking and eating at the same time.
He's just missed the bus.
He is enjoying his meal at home.
```

278 **Variation** The sentences may not be true or false but may be judged subjectively as more or less appropriate.

279 **Variation** One picture and three descriptive texts are given to each student. Each text contains true and false information related to the picture. The student must read all three texts, decide what is true and what is false and then write out a true text.

Note Someone must write the three texts! This could be done by more advanced students for the less advanced.

Find your partner

280 Classwork. Each student is given one card. On the card there is either a picture or a text. The students must walk around the class looking for the picture to match their text or vice versa. Texts can be: names, descriptions, definitions, descriptions of functions, associations, titles of pictures, captions.

Or the picture might represent the first part of a sentence and the text the second part of the sentence.

167

Newspaper photographs and articles

281 Groupwork. Several newspaper photographs are given to the students to discuss what they might represent. Then several related texts are given to the students; these may be quite difficult but the gist should be clear to the students. The students then match the photographs to the articles. Afterwards the students can be asked to say what 'clues' they used in the articles and photographs.

282 **Variation** Use advertisement pictures and texts.

Picture postcards of places

283 Groupwork. Several postcards and, separately, several texts taken from postcards are given to the students. The students must decide which text is most likely to have been written with each picture.

Ambiguous pictures

284 Classwork or groupwork. Several ambiguous pictures and more texts than there are pictures are given to the students. The students must decide which text is the most appropriate for each picture.

You can make ambiguous pictures by cutting out part of a picture so that it is difficult to identify and interpret.

Family tree

285 Groupwork or individual work. A family tree with missing information is given to the students. The students study it and may like to discuss the idea of family trees. Then they listen to or read a text and fill in the missing details. Afterwards, the students can draw their own family tree.

Friends and acquaintances

286 Individual work. The students are given a number of illustrations of faces on a piece of paper. They listen to or read a text and draw in lines between the people which show whether they are friends or not.

A story and a picture

287 Groupwork. The students are given a text and a picture which is not necessarily intended to illustrate that text. The students read the text and decide which parts of the text the picture might relate to. They should produce as many ways as possible for the picture to relate to the text.

A story and a film

288 Groupwork and individual work. The students are given a story to read. They are asked to skim read it first of all and are then told that they are film producers and must choose actors and locations for the story. A lot of pictures of people, places and objects are displayed. The various groups of students decide which people and which locations to choose. Afterwards they can present their ideas to the rest of the class.

Poems, stories and pictures

289 Groupwork and individual work. Several poems (or a story) and a lot of pictures are given to the students. The students read the poems and then choose the pictures which they feel best illustrate a particular poem. The pictures can be pasted down on a big piece of paper together with the poem. Alternatively, a collage can be made or a book cover can be designed for the poems or story.

290 **Variation** As the students listen to or read a poem they make a doodle which represents how they feel about it.

10.3 Challenge to group

In these activities the students are given a number of texts and pictures. The texts and/or pictures must be arranged in groups, which may be subjectively or objectively organised.

Arguing for groupings

291 Groupwork. The students are given about twenty cards which have either a picture or a text (from a single word up to a short paragraph) on them. The students are asked to arrange the texts and pictures in several groups and to be ready to argue for each grouping. For example, 'This group is about the countryside, because you can find all of these things in the country.' 'This group is about hope, because we would like to have all of these things!'.

292 **Variation** The same activity can be adapted for special purposes. For example, for engineers the pictures (including diagrams) and texts can relate to different kinds of machines etc.; for economists the pictures (including graphs and tables) and texts can relate to different kinds of statistics.

Countryside

Hope!

Bill Bloggs and Penny Poppy

293 Groupwork. A group of four students is divided into pairs. One pair represents Bill Bloggs, and the other pair Penny Poppy. Each pair is given various texts which indicate the nature of their character. The texts might be specifically written for the activity and/or be authentic items such as tickets, menus, postcards. The students then study their texts and discuss what sort of person their character is.

The group is then given a number of pictures of people, places and objects and asked to divide them up according to whether they might relate to one or other of the people. In order to reach agreement, the two pairs must describe their characters and discuss with each other how the various pictures relate to them. For example, the woman may have been described as an ambitious businesswoman and the man as someone who likes walking in the country. If there are two pictures of cars one might be a smart town car and the other a four-wheel drive country car and these pictures can be allocated appropriately.

294 **Variation** Instead of descriptions of people the texts may describe places, and the students have to sort a number of pictures into groups, each relating to one of the places.

171

295 Variation The students are given several letters describing the interests of various people and they are then given pictures of places and things to do on holiday. They divide the pictures up according to the descriptions of the people's interests.

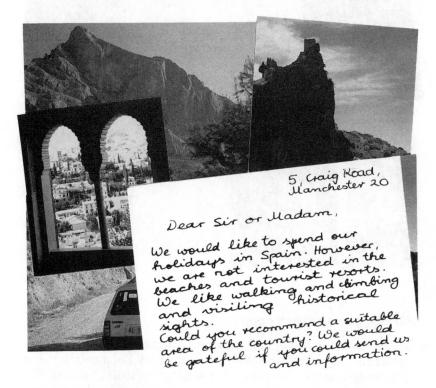

5, Craig Road,
Manchester 20

Dear Sir or Madam,

We would like to spend our holidays in Spain. However, we are not interested in the beaches and tourist resorts. We like walking and climbing and visiting historical sights. Could you recommend a suitable area of the country? We would be grateful if you could send us information.

Formal and informal

296 Groupwork. The students are given a number of pictures (of people, buildings, clothes and other things that can be grouped according to size, shape, etc.) and a number of texts (speech, letters, newspaper articles, etc.). They are asked to divide the texts and pictures into groups according to the formality or informality expressed.

The activity may then be continued by asking the students to match and order the pictures and texts according to levels of formality and informality.

Make a meal

297 Groupwork. The students are given several recipes and a number of pictures of unprepared foods. They arrange the ingredients into groups according to the different recipes.

Shopping

298 Groupwork. The students are given a shopping list and a number of pictures. They arrange the pictures according to the sort of shops where the goods are to be found.

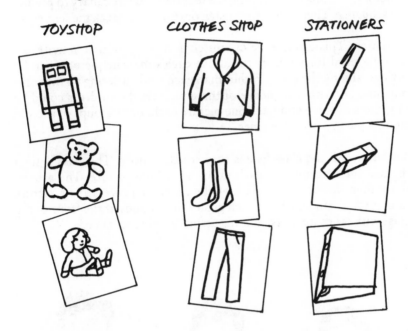

TOYSHOP   CLOTHES SHOP   STATIONERS

10.4 Challenge to sequence

In these activities the students are challenged to put a number of pictures into a sequence. The sequence can be reached independently or can be determined by a text. For example, the students can create their own story by ordering a number of pictures as they wish or, alternatively, they arrange the pictures to match a story provided by the teacher. With the latter technique it can be judged right or wrong. If there is a 'subjective sequence' the students can be asked to explain and justify their sequencing of the pictures. In the selection of activities which follow there are both objective and subjective examples.

General picture sequencing

299 Individual, group or classwork. Several pictures are given to each student. These pictures can be loose or might be reproduced on one sheet of paper. The student listens to or reads a text (it might be a story or

a description of a process) and then puts the pictures into an appropriate sequence. If the pictures are loose the student physically moves them into position. If they are printed on a single sheet the student can write numbers under them.

Before listening to or reading the text the students can try to predict the sequence. Then, while they listen or read, they check the sequence.

300 **Variation** This can also be organised as a group of pair activity. To create a need for students to talk to each other the pictures can be divided among the group rather than each student seeing all the components, i.e. with a sequence of three pictures the students could be in groups of three and have one picture each, or in groups of six and share a picture with a partner.

301 **Variation** All the class listens to or reads a story. The class is then divided into groups and each group is given a picture. The groups must then decide which part of the story or process their picture illustrates. A student from each group then stands at the front of the class with other students, holding up pictures in sequence.

A gap story

302 Class, group, or individual work. The students see a picture (or pictures) and a text with gaps (on the board, overhead projector or on individual student sheets). The students complete the text by referring to the pictures.

Random picture story

303 Class, group, or individual work. The teacher displays ten to twenty pictures on the walls of the classroom. He or she then invents a story which makes reference to each picture. The pictures can be taken in any order. The teacher can point to the appropriate picture or leave the students to guess which picture he or she is referring to. It is advisable to give each picture a number. As they listen, the students note down the sequence of pictures they think the teacher has chosen.

Film symphony

304 Class, or groupwork. In this activity the students choose pictures to represent the characters, important objects and locations in a story (see below for how to organise the activity). They also follow the experiences of each character through the story by drawing a line on a graph. The line rises or falls as the character becomes tense or relaxed.

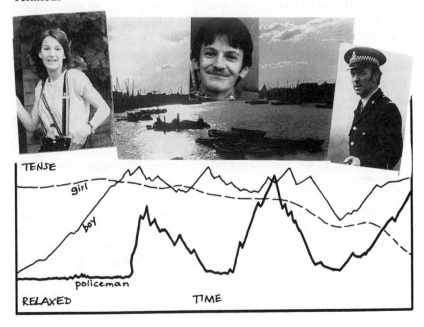

Alternatively, the lines can be drawn without the graph and can be shown moving closer to each other or further away according to how the characters relate to each other.

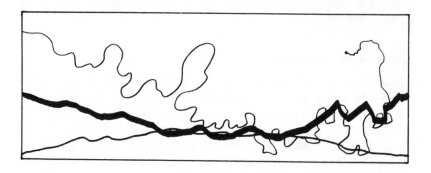

The quality of the line can be used to show whether the character is nervous, angry, gentle, etc. Numbers can be written on the graph at certain points, which can be key points in the text. Quotations and notes on intonation and register patterns can be written below the graph.

There are various approaches to organising this activity. One way would be as follows for a written text:

Each student is given a text of a story to read for homework. The students are asked to be familiar with the story line, the nature of the characters and the places where the story takes place. The students are then asked to work in small groups (four). They are given a number of magazine pictures of people, objects and places. They discuss which pictures to use to illustrate the story (as if they were researching for a film). The students then draw one (or all) of the graphs and flow-charts to represent their interpretation of the story.

When this stage has been completed the groups are divided. Two students remain with their choice of pictures and their graphs and flowcharts. The other two students go to another group and ask questions and guess who and what their pictures, graphs and flowcharts represent.

305 **Variation** Individual and pairwork. A simple variation is for the students to listen to or read a story and then to look at a range of pictures displayed by the teacher. Each student chooses pictures he or she feels illustrate aspects of the story. The students then work in pairs and explain why they have chosen the pictures. The students could, of course, draw illustrations themselves, write down key parts of the text next to them and draw story graphs.

176

10.5 Challenge to order

In these activities the students are asked to order a number of pictures according to their view of the quality or suitability of the objects represented in the pictures: their evaluation is based on a text.

Cars

306 Group or pairwork. Pictures of cars and information about them are given to the students together with pictures and information about various people. The students arrange the pictures of the cars in order of suitability for each person.

```
VW POLO 1100

Length       3.82m
Width        1.61m
Tank         8.9 gallons
MPG          40
Top speed    87mph

Economical 3 door hatchback
```

```
Tom Taylor

Electrician, self employed
Hobby, fishing
Wife, Elaine (35) nursery teacher
Two children, 13 and 8
```

Advertisements

307 Group or pairwork. A number of advertisements for the same or similar products are shown to the students. The students read the texts and listen to the teacher talking about the products and the potential buyers. The students then put the advertisements in order of their likely appeal to the buyers.

177

Holidays

308 Group or pairwork. The students are given brief biographical details about a holiday maker, their interests and limitations in terms of time and money. They then look at information about several holiday places and put them in order of preference for the person described.

10.6 Challenge to memorise

In these activities, the students are challenged to remember the detail or gist of a text and then to demonstrate what they remember by doing something non-verbal. What the students do will involve one of the other challenges described in this book. The students might, for example, draw or arrange pictures in a sequence, point to particular pictures or parts of pictures or underline false statements. The various activities described under 'Challenge to sequence' could be combined with 'Challenge to memorise' if the text is only available to the students for a limited time.

Remembering a picture

309 Individual and pairwork. The students are given, for a short time only, a written (or oral) description of a picture, diagram or map. They then attempt to draw the picture from memory, first of all individually and then by comparing their drawing with their neighbour's drawing.

Pointing and encircling

310 Individual and pairwork. The students read a text or hear an extract and are then given a picture, diagram or map. From memory the students point at what was referred to, ring a number of things in the picture, or draw a route on the map, which they then compare with their neighbour.

Underlining

311 Individual or groupwork. The students are shown a picture (or a sequence of pictures) for a short time. They are then given a text about it, some parts of which are incorrect. If the text is written, the students must read it and underline the statements which are not true. If the text is spoken they must raise their hands when they hear something which is not true. The picture should be shown again at the end so the students can see how well they have remembered it.

Pelmanism

12 Groupwork. Two sets of cards are needed: one set is pictures and the other set is words or sentences describing or related to the pictures. Both sets of cards are turned upside down and placed randomly on a table. The students try to remember the position of the matching cards. They then take it in turns to turn over two cards. If the two cards are a matching pair (picture of an apple and the word apple) the student 'keeps' them. If they don't match he or she turns them over again. (This can also be played in teams, which makes the game just as competitive but less threatening.)

11 Communication and opportunities

'Opportunities' comprises a richer section in Part B Emphasis on speaking and writing. Non-verbal opportunities to do things related to pictures and texts are more limited.

11.1 Opportunity to imagine

Pictures in the mind

313 Individual and pairwork. The teacher describes people, places or objects in terms of appearance and behaviour. The students listen, and afterwards they tell each other what they saw or draw and describe it. If students have not made use of this potentially rich idea before it is a good idea to begin with the simplest of descriptions, like this:

Teacher: I am going to ask you to close your eyes and then I am going to name something. I want to find out if you can see it in your mind. Close your eyes. It's a tree. Have a good look at it for a few moments. Now open your eyes.

The teacher then asks the students a number of questions.

Teacher: Was it a big tree? Were there leaves on the tree? Did you see anything else near the tree?

The description can be given in more detail when the students have got used to the idea.

Teacher: Close your eyes. There is a tree. It is a big tree. Go closer to the tree. Feel its trunk. Is it rough or smooth? What colour is the bark? Now, stand back from the tree. It is summer and there are leaves on the tree. Is there a breeze? Are the leaves moving?

Once the students are familiar with the idea a story can be told in the same way. Teachers who use this technique sometimes play music as they talk to the students.

If the students are asked to describe what they have seen and to discuss it with other students the activity becomes a productive one.

However, the activity has great potential purely as a listening opportunity. It is free from stress for the students precisely because they are not asked to do anything which may expose them.

Illustrating and designing

14 Individual work. The students read or listen to a text and then draw a picture which illustrates part of it, or design a page, symbol or motif which they feel would be appropriate for it.

Over misted blue hills and distant water
In chaing-nan at autumns end
the grass has not yet wilted.
By night on the Four-and-Twenty Bridges,
under the full moon,
where are you teaching a jade girl
to blow tunes on your flute?

For most teachers pictures are a cheap and readily available resource. Furthermore, students are usually very willing to contribute pictures to the class collection. The problem is what to do with them. This part of the book attempts to help the teacher to think of effective ways of using any type of picture material. Sources of pictures are listed and discussed in chapter 12, and in chapters 13 and 14 suggestions are made about what to do with them. In chapter 15 suggestions are given for creating and adapting pictures, and in chapter 16 about how to file pictures.

12   Sources of pictures

In many countries there is an abundance of pictures. The language teacher can, with little effort, build up an enormous picture library. In all countries it is possible to find at least some free or cheap picture material.

Students themselves can be asked to bring pictures for the picture library. In secondary schools of 2,000 students that could mean 2,000 pictures if they each brought one!

Newspapers

Pictures in newspapers are not reproduced very well. However, old newspapers are available everywhere and in some countries are the main source of free picture material. Cartoon strips are particularly useful. The pictures in newspapers are usually small and too indistinct for use with the whole class, but they are usually topical and linked with text, which can lead to particular activities. The pictures can be cut out and the text rejected, or the text (captions and articles) can be retained and used in matching activities (for example, see Activities 280, 281).

Magazines

In many countries these are the major source of useful picture material of a high quality, though they are rarely free. In some

182

countries they may be a source even though the printing quality may not be very good and there may not be a great range of types of picture. Full page pictures are big enough for class use, while others are more appropriate for individual work.

Teachers are usually familiar with general magazines, but may be less familiar with specialist magazines which are often a source of some fascinating pictures, for example, a small boy holding up a gigantic fish that he has caught (taken from a fishing magazine). Specialist magazines can be a source of pictures for teachers of languages for special purposes.

Radio and television programme guides are often illustrated. The small pictures, which often illustrate films and/or famous people, are useful for individual work. The pictures can be cut out and filed separately from the text, or kept together for matching activities (see Activities 280, 281) or grouped thematically for topic work (see pages 111 and 112).

Advertisements and publicity

These include direct mail leaflets, posters, and advertisements in magazines and newspapers. Sizes vary, making the pictures of use in both classwork and groupwork. There are two features which make advertisement pictures special:

1. The pictures are meant to persuade us to buy the product. This means that the product is usually presented to us in an unreal way. People in advertisements usually look like actors or models (which is what they are) pretending to be normal people. If the teacher shows a picture advertising a man's suit and asks what the man is thinking and what sort of man he is, etc. (see Activity 195 for the use of ambiguous pictures), then the real answer must be that he is wondering whether he is showing the best view of his face or if his fee is big enough.

   Thus, on the whole, it is better to use advertisement pictures for describing rather than for interpreting.

2. Advertisement pictures are nearly always accompanied by text which provides authentic material for reading. The type of advertising copy will determine the most appropriate exploitation, e.g. scanning to find the supplier's address or intensive reading of 'small print'.

   The text can be removed or retained, either with or without the picture. If the text is kept, it can be used with the picture for matching activities (see, for example, Activity 282), or for topic work (see pages 111 and 112).

G

Holiday brochures

These brochures are usually richly illustrated. Most of the pictures are of hotels, but many are of places, historical sites or places of great beauty. There are specialist holiday brochures for people who like activity holidays and these might be of more interest to the language teacher as they contain pictures of people climbing, taking photographs, painting, studying insects, etc. The pictures are usually only big enough for individual work.

These pictures can be cut out and filed under, for example, 'places' or 'activities'. However, the teacher might like to keep some holiday brochures complete for topic work: the sorts of ways people take holidays, the advantages and disadvantages of types of holiday, etc. (see pages 111 and 112, and Activities 156, 157, 294, 295, 308).

Business brochures

Many businesses produce brochures so their customers and the public know about the services they offer. Banks and post offices can be a good source of publicity pictures. Even universities and colleges produce brochures and it is possible to find pictures of students reading, writing, talking or relaxing. Such brochures might be of particular use to teachers of language for special purposes. They can be kept complete for topic work (see pages 111 and 112), or the pictures may be cut out and filed separately.

Catalogues

In some countries catalogues are an amazingly rich source of picture material. In Britain there are catalogues with literally thousands of pictures of every sort of object which a big store can sell, from beds and bicycles to books. There are also specialist catalogues, for example, of toys, cars or gifts, and charity catalogues might be a source of pictures for teachers of languages for special purposes. The individual pictures can be cut out and filed under their subject or the teacher might decide to keep the pages complete in order to simulate the feeling of choice for the students which is so characteristic of a catalogue (for example, see Activities 261, 271, 306).

Calendars

Calendars are usually illustrated and, furthermore, the pictures are usually big enough for class use. Sometimes it may be an advantage to keep the calendar dates.

Greetings cards

Most greetings cards are illustrated. The range of subjects is very wide, and in every case the illustration has been chosen to 'say' something to the receiver. It is often worth keeping the text and the picture together. There are greetings cards for: various seasonal celebrations, wishing people well if they are ill, congratulating them on a success, etc.

Postcards

Every possible subject is illustrated on postcards. Postcards are associated with writing and thus postcards are not just pictures. When the picture on the card is of a particular place, for example, a picture of the colleges at Cambridge, then a text can be given or invented by the students as if written there.

Two great advantages of the postcard are that they are made of card and all postcards are about the same size. It is worth keeping all postcards of places together and separate from other pictures of places because of this connection with writing. Postcard pictures can also be filed according to what they depict, for example, transport, art, people.

Reproductions of art

Paintings, drawings and art photographs are reproduced on postcards, greetings cards, calendars, in books and as separate reproductions available in shops and galleries.

Paintings, sculpture and art photography represent an immense range of objects, scenes and abstract concepts. The reproductions could therefore be filed under these. However, the special quality of art is that it is expressive and stimulating, and so reproductions of art should probably be filed together and used mainly for creative work (for example, see Activities 178, 179, 200, 232).

Posters

Posters are designed to be big enough to be seen from a distance and they are thus ideal for class use. Posters can be advertisements or just intended for decoration. A huge poster may show one object or it may illustrate a lot of information.

Posters displayed in a language teaching room can contribute to a feeling of the foreign culture.

Advertisement posters can often be obtained free by writing to the

185

firm that produced them and saying that the poster will be used in a college or school. Posters for decorative use are not usually free, but they are often inexpensive. The easiest way of keeping posters is to fold them neatly and keep them in a file or drawer.

Wallcharts

Wallcharts are produced by some institutions to explain what is done in or by the institution: how steel is made, how a firm exports around the world, how to grow rice, how to deal with a road accident, the journey of a letter. Very often these wallcharts are free or relatively inexpensive. If the teacher is working in a college or school where other subjects are taught it might be possible to borrow a wallchart.

The easiest way of storing wallcharts is to fold them neatly and keep them in a file or drawer. Wallcharts can be used in identifying activities (for example, Activities 69, 71, 86, 87), matching activities (see Activities 144, 269) and memorising (see Activities 166, 167).

Instructions

Instructions for carrying out a process such as cooking or putting on a life jacket are often illustrated. They can be used in sequencing activities (for example, see Activities 127, 299, 301).

Old books

It is a shame to throw away a book if it contains illustrations. Old children's books are a particularly good source of illustrations which can often charm older students. Old school books are often too decrepit or dated to keep, but they may contain unique illustrations. This can be a particularly rich source for teachers of language for special purposes.

Comics and cartoon strips

These are heavily illustrated. They are sequences of pictures which are closely related to a narrative text. The stories in some publications are illustrated by hundreds of photographs. (For sequencing, see Activities 110, 111, 112, 113, 114, 119, 122, 124, 125, 224, 301.)

Family photographs and slides

Sometimes family photographs can be brought to the lesson, shown and talked about. We all have photographs and slides which we do not really want to keep and never look at (and that applies to our students as well).

Stamps

Most stamps have pictures on them. The most obvious way of using stamps is to talk about them as stamps: where they come from, why the designs were chosen, how much they are worth, etc. However, they can also be stuck onto separate cards and used as 'playing' cards for groupwork.

Playing cards

Many playing cards have illustrations. The cards can be used for their original purpose and the students asked to play the game in the target language. However, the cards can also be used for the pictures that are on them.

Wrapping paper

Wrapping paper is often decorated with pictures. The repetition of the design means that pairs of pictures are available. (See Activities 60, 62, 171.)

Coursebook

There are usually illustrations in the coursebook. These illustrations can often be used in ways which the author does not suggest.

The teacher's and students' own drawings

Of course, it is very useful if the teacher is a talented artist or if there is a talented artist in the class. However, it is not necessary to be artistically talented in order to produce pictures. Pictures can be drawn on the board, the overhead projector, large paper, flashcards, group playing cards, handout sheets, or collage sheets (see chapter 15).

Photocopying

Pictures can be photocopied but, if they are in copyright, only by permission. Some countries have schemes whereby schools can acquire a blanket licence for photocopying. In other countries permission should be obtained from the copyright holder.

However, the photocopying machine may be used by the teacher to make pictures, for example, by photocopying objects such as keys, tickets, etc.

13 What to do with a picture

Teachers often feel dismayed when they open a magazine and see all the pictures inside. They know that pictures are useful and they realise that the pictures in the magazine are free . . . but how do they use them? In this chapter and the next there are suggestions which are designed to help teachers who feel that their minds are a 'complete blank'! But before offering suggestions some assurances should be given.

- The teacher will very often feel that his or her idea is not very good and that a really creative person would have a better idea. Everyone feels this at some time. The suggestions which follow provide every teacher with some basically useful ideas, and that is what matters.
- It is often more productive and more enjoyable to think up ideas with other teachers or with the students themselves or even with friends than working alone.
- Although there are many suggestions in the pages that follow it is most important that the teacher values him or herself. A personal reaction to a picture is more likely to interest the teacher and the students than one adopted from someone else.

13.1 Personal response

It is important to remind the teacher that he or she is an individual first of all, rather than just a teacher! It would be a pity if the teacher followed a set of guidelines evolved by someone else without first of all responding to a picture or pictures in an individual way. The teacher should listen to his or her own internal voice when looking at a picture. 'Stop thinking about your teaching for a few moments and think about the picture and what you feel about it.'

When I see this sort of advertisement I always find myself wondering which book I would like to have. My internal voice says, 'Which book would I like? This one . . . or perhaps that one. Isn't that a good way to make use of this picture, saying which book I would like and asking students which book they would like to have?'

188

What to do with a picture

189

Here is another picture:

My internal voice says, 'I wonder who lives there? I wonder where it is? It looks like part of England. It could be the North East but it could be . . . '

Advertisements which offer a variety of goods of the same kind encourage our inner voice to say 'would like', 'wouldn't like' and 'which one' and 'this one'. Pictures which are mysterious invite speculation. My inner voice naturally uses the language of speculation: 'wonder', 'could', 'might'. In each case the first idea for using these pictures comes from listening to my inner voice. The inner voice leads to a natural and authentic use of language.

Unfortunately, my inner voice is often silent or just mumbles! What should the teacher do if no idea suggests itself? At this point it is useful to have a way of categorising pictures and being aware of the kind of activity which can be done with them (see page 193).

13.2 Pictures which illustrate

Some pictures seem to illustrate an object, action, quality, etc. very clearly. It is almost as if that is what the picture was intended for. Such pictures are usually very simple with the minimum background and the minimum of extra bits of information.

Stools   Chairs

Pictures which seem to highlight a particular concept can be used for the teaching of meaning. However, it should be noted that a single picture cannot usually teach a new meaning unambiguously. It may be necessary, for example, to have several pictures of the same object in order to focus the students' minds on the concept concerned. For more ideas on the teaching of meaning, see page 136.

Pictures which illustrate certain concepts clearly can also be used for cueing answers to questions and for making substitutions in sentences.
Question and answer work:
Teacher: Where's the mouse?
Student: It's in the cup.

The picture can also be used in simulated conversations:
Teacher: (*holding up a picture of a pear*). Would you like a pear?
Student: (*picking up a picture of an apple*) No, thank you. I'd rather have an apple.

Sometimes it is effective to choose a picture which highlights a simple concept but is at the same time an extraordinary picture. For example, 'eating': the picture could be of a monster eating.

For more ideas on mini-dialogues see page 116, and for mechanical practice see pages 18 and 22.

H

13.3 Pictures which imply

Some words and structures might be implied by a picture even though they are not specifically illustrated.

In this illustration it is easy to guess that the man is in a restaurant and has just finished eating.

For the use of pictures which imply a word or structure, see ideas on the teaching of meaning, page 136, and mini-dialogues, page 116.

14 Types of picture and types of use

14.1 Checkchart for pictures

Use the checkchart to stimulate ideas for particular ways of using pictures you have found. If a special idea occurs, write it on the back of the picture or on an envelope and keep the picture in it. If no special idea occurs, file the picture in the general subject file (see page 212).

Examples of activities which make use of the different types of pictures are given and referred to by their activity number. It is most important that these are not seen as exclusive. The same pictures can often be used for purposes other than those listed here. Indeed, with imagination, pictures can be used in such a variety of ways that no definitive guide could be given.

14.2 Pictures of single objects

Many of the activities described in this book make use of pictures showing a single object.

General things to talk about:

Food: appearance; naming; preferences; comparing foods of the same type; countable and uncountable; cost; origin; containers; weight; how to cook; good or bad for health.

Clothes: appearance; naming; preferences; suitability; cost; fashion.

Cars: naming the manufacturer; country of manufacture; performance; appropriacy for different kinds of people; appearance; cost; comparisons.

Animals: appearance; naming; habitat; characteristics; rarity; relationship with people; comparisons.

Everyday objects: naming; possession; cost; usefulness; purpose and appropriateness; unusual uses; comparisons.

Gifts: naming; preference for self and for others; appropriateness; cost.

For some examples of the use of pictures of single objects, see ideas on

WHAT TO DO WITH A PICTURE: INVENTING

PAGES 188 to 203

FIRST OF ALL SEE
HOW YOUR OWN MIND
RESPONDS TO THE PICTURE.
IF YOU CAN, ASK YOUR FRIENDS
AND STUDENTS AS WELL. YOU
MIGHT DECIDE TO KEEP SOME
OF THE TEXT .....
THEN CUT IT OUT...

FILING

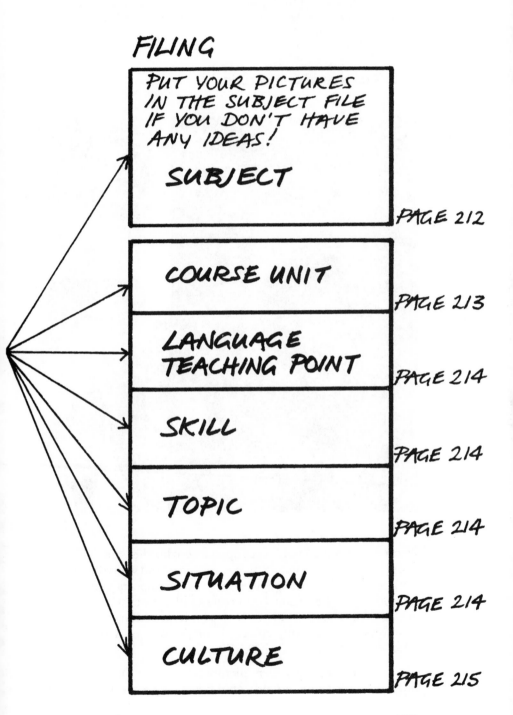

PUT YOUR PICTURES
IN THE SUBJECT FILE
IF YOU DON'T HAVE
ANY IDEAS!

SUBJECT

PAGE 212

COURSE UNIT

PAGE 213

LANGUAGE
TEACHING POINT

PAGE 214

SKILL

PAGE 214

TOPIC

PAGE 214

SITUATION

PAGE 214

CULTURE

PAGE 215

the teaching of meaning, page 136, and mini-dialogues, page 116.
(Also, see Activities 4, 41, 63, 77, 101, 106, 153, 162, 199, 207, 212,
217, 243, 257, 260, 273, 298.)

14.3 Pictures of one person

Pictures of people invite us to speculate who they are, what sort of
people they are (age, family, work, concerns) and what they are thinking and feeling. In these pictures the action is important only in telling
us more about the person. For pictures with actions which are important in themselves, see Pictures of people in action, page 197. (For
examples of the use of pictures of one person, see Activities 40, 78,
143, 145, 195, 220, 223, 225, 270, 276, 286.)

Note A lot of advertisement pictures show a single person, but it is
difficult to speculate seriously about them as people because they are

obviously models. Such pictures are best used as a representation of the object being sold rather than as an example of a person.

14.4 Pictures of famous people

General things to talk about:
Identify: reason for fame; achievement; evaluation of what they have done/are doing/will do.
Character: background (origin, influence, struggles, etc.); physical description; like/dislike/admire.
Would you like to be that person? Role play the person; pretend to interview the person.
(For example, see Activities 70, 209.)

14.5 Pictures of several people

General things to do and to talk about:
Speech and thought bubbles cut out of sticky paper can be stuck on the picture. Students imagine what the people might be saying and thinking. There is often an opportunity to discuss aspects of register and function according to the nature of the people, their apparent relationship and the setting they are in. For example, see Activities 51, 221, 222.

14.6 Pictures of people in action

General things to talk about:
Everyday activities: describing and naming; what they are saying and/ or thinking and feeling; commenting on the people and their actions; giving personal attitude/relationship to/experience of the activity; functions, for example, apologising, persuading, complaining, explaining.
What has happened before the action? What will hapapen next? Conversations before and after.
Sport, hobbies and entertainment: describing and naming; preferences; evaluating; comparing.
Work: describing and naming; preferences; evaluating; comparing.
Travel and transport: describing and naming; evaluating in relation to appropriacy; cost, etc.; personal experience.
Situations: accidents; why; how; personal experience; what to do; precautions.
(For example, see Activities 6, 18, 83, 84, 203, 213, 235, 236, 263.)

14.7   Pictures of places

Pictures of places might include: home or abroad; landscapes; townscapes; single buildings; views.

General things to talk about:

Where is it? When was the picture taken? How do you know? What sort of place is it (geological, climatic, social, historical aspects)?

Preferences: personal experiences; been there or somewhere similar?; comparing; evaluating in relation to certain professions; life styles, etc.

How to get there? Who to go with? Why go there?

Buildings: describing and naming; purpose; appearance; history; comparing with home.

(For example, see Activities 45, 49, 92, 143, 156, 198, 204, 211, 275, 283, 294, 295, 308.)

14.8   Pictures from history

Pictures illustrating scenes, costumes and objects from history can be used like other pictures but have the additional quality of inviting the use of past tense forms. They can be used in personal evaluation: would you like to have lived then? (For example, see Activity 200.)

14.9   Pictures with a lot of information

Some pictures are full of information. There may be a lot of people doing different things, or it may be a landscape or cityscape showing lots of objects, buildings, etc. The complexity of some pictures makes them particularly suitable for some activities:

'Describe and identify' activities in which someone describes part of

198

the picture and other students decide which part it is. (For example, see Activities 69, 70, 71, 74.)

'Matching' activities, for example, true/false games in which someone makes a statement which is true or false and other students decide which it is. (For example, see Activities 85, 86, 87.)

'Memory' activities in which students try to remember as much as they can of a picture. (For example, see Activities 164, 165, 166, 167.)

14.10 Pictures of the news

News pictures invite identification of the incident, what happened, where, when, and to whom. They are normally linked with captions and articles, and it is usually a good idea to retain the texts even if they will not be read in detail. Texts can be read for gist and then matched up with one of a number of similar pictures. (For example, see Activities 42, 141, 142, 281.)

14.11 Pictures of fantasies

Fantasy pictures can be cut out of old children's books. They often illustrate everyday activities, for example, eating, sleeping, running, etc., even if the characters are from the world of fantasy. Sometimes it is amusing to teach the words for these basic concepts through an unusual or amusing picture. Such pictures can also be used in story-telling. (For example, see Activities 181, 195, 302, 303, 305.)

14.12 Pictures of maps and symbols

Pictures of symbols can be found in road traffic booklets, holiday brochures, etc.

General things to talk about:

What does the symbol mean? How do you know? What should you do? What shouldn't you do? What have you got to do? What can you do/see/get there? (For example, see Activities 54, 152, 247, 256.)

What can you recognise on the map? What would you see if you were to follow a certain route? (For example, see Activities 147, 148, 265, 310.)

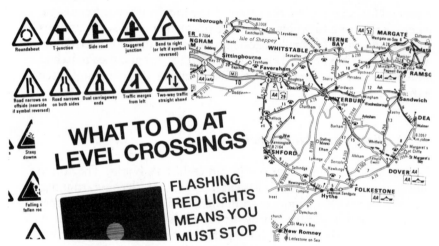

14.13 Pairs of pictures

Pairs of pictures are always useful. (Two copies of the same issue of a magazine will provide pairs of pictures.) (For example, see Activities 60, 61, 62, 171.) Pictures which are similar, rather than identical, can also be used in matching activities. The students must describe the differences between them. (For example, see Activities 81, 82.)

14.14 Pictures and texts

Some pictures have captions or articles accompanying them: cartoons, newspaper pictures, advertisements, pictures cut out of old books, etc., and it is a shame to throw the text away. Even if the text is above the productive level of the students it could be used for reading for gist. Consider retaining the texts and sticking them on a separate piece of card. (For example, see Activities 280, 281, 287, 291, 292, 312.)

14.15 Sequences of pictures

Cartoon strips and instruction strips of pictures are potentially useful. Experience will show the teacher which strips are the most useful. The strips can be kept as they are and used to contextualise a story or description of a process. First of all the teacher can ask questions to help the students grasp the meaning of the strip. Intermediate and advanced students can discuss the technique of the cartoonist in his or her representation of the people and setting and the relationship between the drawing and the words.

Strips can be used to stimulate and guide writing (for example, see Activities 110, 111, 112, 113, 114, 119, 122, 125). Or they can be cut up and given to different students who work out the story or process (for example, see Activities 124, 301).

14.16 Related pictures

Pictures which are related to each other can be treated as separate pictures and used in mini-dialogues, etc. However, they can also be kept together and provide a basis for topic work involving a variety of skills. Themes might include: advertising, fashion, holidays, the culture of the foreign country (see pages 111 and 112).

Holiday catalogues can be kept complete and used as authentic material rather than as separate pictures. Students can be asked to find the sort of information that would be needed to choose and plan a holiday: reasons for going to a place, costs, times, etc. (For example, see Activities 92, 93, 156, 157, 275, 283.)

Related pictures can also be used in various 'grouping' activities (for example, see Activities 92, 93, 99, 101, 103, 105, 291, 297, 298) and in 'ordering' activities (for example, see Activities 153, 154, 158, 306, 307).

14.17 Single stimulating pictures

Some photographs show images of people in their environment with great sensitivity, which can stimulate speculation (see page 109) and the expression of experiences and feelings (see page 99). This can lead to storytelling (for example, see Activities 130, 135, 136, 143, 144, 145, 150, 151).

14.18 Ambiguous pictures

Some pictures are difficult to understand. It might be difficult to recognise what the picture represents or what is happening. Different interpretations give reasons for speaking and listening. (For example, see Activities 180, 195, 304, 305.)

14.19 Bizarre pictures

Bizarre pictures engage people's attention for a few moments but then tend to become boring because it is difficult to relate to them. The teacher must set a task in order to retain the students' attention. The students can speculate about what is happening (see Activities 180, 195, 196, 197, 199), fit the picture into a story (see Activities 111, 114, 115, 116, 117, 130, 136, 140, 143, 150, 151), match possible textual explanations (see Activities 280, 281, 284, 287, 289), or guess what picture the teacher is holding (see Activities 69, 70, 71, 72, 73).

14.20 Explanatory pictures

Pictures taken from specialist publications or old school books often explain a process. Educational wallcharts are produced by many major firms and these are often given free of charge to schools and colleges.

A picture or wallchart can be looked at while the students read or listen to a passage, and can help the students to grasp the meaning of the text. A simplified copy of the picture can be written on and drawn on by the students as they understand the various stages in the process. Alternatively, the students can be asked to point to different parts of it as they listen to the explanation. Groups can take it in turns to study the picture or wallchart and to work out from the picture what they understand of the text, what the process is, and how it works stage by stage. The interpretations of the different groups can then be compared. (For example, see Activities 299, 300, 301, 302.)

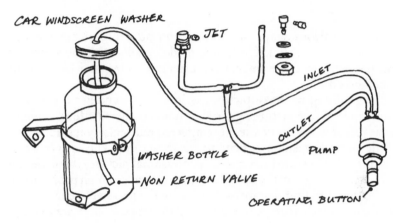

14.21 Student and teacher drawings

The students and teacher can draw pictures which could substitute most, if not all, of the pictures listed above. And that is their main purpose: they provide an immediately available source of pictorial material for the activities. Student and teacher drawings also have a special quality, which lies in their immediacy and their individuality. For this reason they are suitable as illustrations for personal expression. (For example, see Activities 185, 186, 187, 190, 202, 229, 230, 242, 248, 252, 253, 255, 258, 262, 264, 267, 268, 272, 274, 290, 314.) For help in producing simple drawings, see the next chapter.

15 Creating and adapting pictures

There are various ways of creating and adapting pictures which increase their potential. The 'home-made' quality stimulates interest and goodwill, and the images are usually striking and likely to be remembered.

Being willing to make pictures is important whether there is an abundance of free picture material or not. Teacher-made or student-made pictures always create more interest, particularly if spiced with a little mirth. But isn't it difficult to create pictures? The answer is that it is difficult to create high quality professional pictures if you do not have the training. On the other hand, the absence of high professional quality is more than compensated for by the goodwill generated by the sight of teacher-made or student-made images. There are two tips which might be helpful:
1. Neatness in picture making is much less important than enjoying the material while creating the picture.
2. A sketchy style is usually less successful than a style which is positive in its use of lines and distinct shapes, even if these are not professionally drawn.

15.1 Simple drawing

Many actions can be represented by simple stick drawings of people.

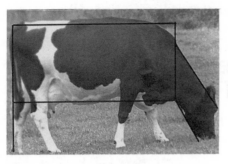

COMPARE THE PROPORTIONS OF THE LEGS AND THE BODY →

COMPARE THE LENGTH OF THE HEAD AND NECK WITH THE BODY

Look for a rectangle which encloses the main shape of the object or animal. Once you have got the proportions of the rectangle correct you have got the main character.
Then it is relatively easy to add details either for a simple blackboard drawing or for a naturalistic drawing.

A simple geometrical shape can usually be found in the most complicated of objects. Once this has been found and its proportions judged, the variations on that shape can be drawn in.

A BASIC BLACKBOARD COW!

MAKE THEM RUN BY OPENING THE LEGS

STAGES IN DRAWING A BICYCLE

205

Scenes can be drawn without the use of linear perspective.

15.2 Pictures on the board

The teacher and/or the students can draw on the board without preparation, and images on it are immediately visible to the whole class. A great advantage of the board is that a picture can grow before one's eyes and parts can be erased and substituted. This flexibility lends itself to cueing for various types of practice or provides a creative stimulus for more open, communicative work, for example, in storytelling (see Activities 52, 57, 66, 128, 129, 131, 132, 134, 137, 249, 258, 262, 264, 267, 268).

15.3 Pictures on the overhead projector

The OHP really does offer tremendous scope to the picture maker! Transparencies can be prepared beforehand by freehand drawing, photocopying or by tracing. Overlay transparencies can also be prepared: these can add or obliterate information for cueing responses in practice activities or for stimulating more open communicative work.

Objects can be put on the OHP, including cardboard cutouts or natural objects, for example, grass or a glass bowl of water. An effect of sunrise and sunset can be achieved by pulling the hand slowly across the lens. In these ways the most imaginative and striking effects can be achieved, and these are wonderful for storytelling and drama. (For example, see Activities 1, 5, 34, 35, 36, 37, 44, 48, 66, 67, 69, 71, 73, 162, 166, 199.)

15.4 Paper and card

Paper and card are usually available to the teacher, and felt tip pens give immense scope for the production of pictures. Colour, however, should be used with some consideration for its purpose. Drawings can be freehand or may be traced onto card.

Pictures can be of single objects or may be larger and more complicated wall pictures. Teacher-made examples of both types are illustrated in this book.

15.5 Collage

Details of people and objects can be cut out of pictures and stuck onto other pictures or stuck onto a piece of card together with other pictures. This way of making pictures allows the teacher to illustrate teaching points in an imaginative and dynamic manner. It also allows the teacher to create a picture which illustrates exactly what he or she wants.

Collage collection

Various objects and animals can be stuck onto a large piece of paper to make a big picture, for example, of a zoo or a street scene or a display of gifts (see Activities 41, 77, 106, 153, 154, 217, 297).

Juxtaposition of pictures

Various pictures which show different aspects of a theme can be stuck on the same sheet of paper, or the pictures can be temporarily placed next to each other on the board using Blu-Tack or pins. The difference between the pictures stimulates discussion (see Activity 173).

Personal collage

A great variety of pictures and realia (tickets, letters, personal photos, etc.) can be stuck on a card or piece of paper. The students can write about themselves or they can base a story on the collage (see Activities 182, 183, 184).

Poetry collage

One or two pictures can be stuck on a piece of paper to present a personal experience. The students can write a poem to go with it (see Activity 181).

209

Story collage

Several pictures can be stuck on a piece of paper either as a sequence or as a single picture collage. The students can write a story to go with it. (For example, see Activities 181, 184, 221, 222, 224.)

15.6 Adapting magazine pictures

Pictures, diagrams and symbols

A picture (or pictures) can be stuck on a piece of paper, and lines, arrows, circles, etc. or other symbols drawn on in order to illustrate a language point. Extra features can also be drawn onto photographs. As every child knows it is possible to draw moustaches on faces! (For example, see Activities 276, 286, 310.)

Cutting up pictures

If a picture is stuck onto card it can then be cut up into pieces so that it is like a jigsaw. (For example, see Activities 69, 70, 72, 102.)

Holes in pictures

Pictures with holes in can be shown to the students and they can be asked to say what has been cut out.

15.7 Folding pictures

There are many ways of folding and cutting pictures so that the information is controlled (see page 26).

FOLD AND CUT A PICTURE.... GUESS WHAT IS MISSING

CUT FLAP FOLDED BACK

FOLD—

THIS IS JUST ONE OF PIECE OF PAPER!!

16 Filing pictures

The pictures should be filed so that they can be found and used easily. Teachers must develop their own filing system because it should represent their individual needs and circumstances. Most filing systems are modified as they are used, and for these reasons it is not possible to put forward an ideal filing system. Instead, a number of systems used by teachers are described, and one or all of them can be used!

16.1 Filing by subject

Filing by subject does not point to a particular use of the pictures. In that sense it is adaptable, easy to do and allows for multiple use of the same pictures. The subject file is particularly important for those teachers who cannot get hold of many pictures. However, it is important for all teachers in the sense that filing by subject provides easy access to pictures for mini-dialogues (see page 116). A simple filing system might be: People, Food and drink, Objects, Animals and plants, Places.

This simple filing system could be modified as the teacher's collection of pictures grows: People (portraits); People (jobs); People (famous); Sports, hobbies and entertainment; Everyday situations; Unusual situations; News; Historical; Humour; Food and drink; Objects (household); Objects (everyday); Objects (transport); Animals and plants; Places (home); Places (foreign); Places (buildings). Teachers concerned with language for special purposes might develop a filing system which reflects their students' needs and interests. For example, a teacher of English to agricultural students might have files on: Animals (domestic); Animals (vermin); Animals (breeding), etc.

Size of picture

When deciding whether to file a picture for classwork or groupwork the size of the paper is less important than the size of the image. A picture of an apple filling a piece of paper half the size of this page is big enough to be seen from the back of a classroom. A picture which is one metre square may contain details which are impossible to see unless studied at close range. And for most purposes this will mean that such a picture can only be used by groups or individuals. It is usually a good idea to file a picture as one to be used with the whole class or one to be used in groupwork or by individuals, and this does mean that the smallest picture can be useful.

The most practical way of checking the size of a picture intended for class use is to try it out! Basically, a detail which must be recognised from the back of a classroom ought to be at least 3 centimetres in height.

Mini-dialogue cards

Mini-dialogues (see page 116) rely for their success on a plentiful supply of pictures categorised by subject. The teacher should also have a file of mini-dialogue instruction cards or sheets. Mini-dialogue cards can be filed in a shoe box, and sheets can be filed in a ring binder with clear plastic envelopes.

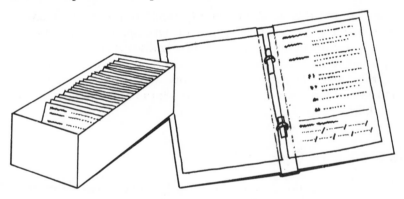

16.2 Filing by course unit

Some teachers file their pictures according to how they can use them in particular units of the course they are doing. The unit file might contain: pictures for controlled oral practice of a new tense form; pictures for writing on the theme of the unit; pictures for the general background of the unit. It is advisable to include notes on how the pictures are to be used.

The advantage of this filing system is that the teacher has everything ready to use. The disadvantage is that the materials may not be so easy to find for revision purposes.

16.3 Filing by language teaching points

It is convenient for many teachers to have a filing system based on the language teaching points of the syllabus they are following. Language teaching points might include functional as well as grammatical points and specific areas of vocabulary.

The files contain pictures which can be used for the presentation and practice stages. It is advisable to include notes on how to use the pictures. Sometimes the picture clearly illustrates the language point, but in other cases it may depend on how the teacher uses the picture and this can be forgotten!

The advantage of this filing system over a course unit filing system is that the language point might occur at several places in the course and with classes of different levels. Filing by language teaching points allows for greater flexibility, including revision.

16.4 Filing by skill

Some pictures prove to be particularly useful for the development of either reading, listening, speaking or writing. For example, an evocative picture of someone in a strange landscape might prove to be very useful for speculation (see Activity 195). A series of four pictures might be particularly successful for story writing (see Activity 130). Pictures and notes for their use can be kept in separate files for the four skills.

16.5 Filing by topic

Filing by topic is not the same as filing by subject. The term 'topic approach', as used here, means the study of a topic in some depth. The student not only learns to master the target language related to the topic but learns about the topic as well (see pages 111 and 112). Topics might include: advertising, art, trade, health and fitness. Any picture or text which relates to the topic would be stored in the file.

16.6 Filing by situation

Many teachers believe that the possible situations for which students might need the foreign language are a central concern in their teaching. Situations might be: travelling (making arrangements, planning, buying tickets, surviving in stations, staying in hotels, etc.), shopping, eating and drinking. Pictures can be filed under these headings.

16.7 Filing by cultural information

Some teachers are particularly concerned about introducing their students to the cultural background of the language they are studying. Pictures which support this aim can be filed separately.

16.8 Protecting and storing pictures

Pictures last longer and look more attractive if they are drawn or mounted on card rather than paper. They look even better and last even longer if they are covered with a self-adhesive transparent plastic.

There are two main considerations for storing pictures. Firstly there is the need to find suitable containers for them, and secondly the need to make the pictures easy to find when they are required.

Pictures can be stored in cardboard boxes with cardboard sheets dividing them into sub-categories. For example, a file based on subjects might have each category of subject divided off by an inter-leaving piece of card.

Pictures of one type should be stored together, for example, all the pictures required for one course unit can be kept in a big envelope. Unit envelopes can themselves be kept in a large cardboard box.

Bibliography

Bassano, Sharon and Christison, Mary Ann, *Drawing Out: Second Language Acquisition through Student-Created Images*, The Alemany Press, 1983.

Chuckney, William, *The Skeleton System*, copublished by Pilgrims Publications, Friendly Press and Hellenic, 1987.

Corder, S. P., 'A Theory of Visual aids', *English Language Teaching Journal*, Vol. 17 No. 2, 1963.

Hansen, A. B., Jones, K., and Legutke, M., 'Interactive Approaches to Fiction', in Peter Olaf Loom and Carl Corensen (eds.), *Practical Classroom Implications*, Sprogsams English Committee and Gesellschaft zur Förderung des Englisch Unterrichts an Gesamtschulen e. V., 1985.

Kerr, J. Y. K., *Picture Cue Cards for Oral Language Practice*, Evans Bros. and Bell Hyman, 1979.

Lockhart, Charles and Woodiwiss, Mary, 'More Activities with Small Cards', *Practical English Teaching*, September 1987.

Maley, Alan and Duff, Alan, *Drama Techniques in Language Learning* (new edition), Cambridge University Press, 1982.

Spaventa, Lou (ed.), *Towards the Creative Teaching of English*, Heinemann Educational, 1987.

Word and Action (Dorset) 1983 Ltd, Dorset BH21 1BS.

Further reading

More examples of the use of pictures in language teaching can be found in the books below:

Bowen, Betty, *Look Here! Visual Aids in Language Teaching*, Macmillan, 1982.

Buckby, Michael and Wright, Andrew, *Flash Cards for Language Learning*, Modern English Publications, a subsidiary of Macmillan Publishers, 1981.

Byrne, Donn, *Teaching Oral English* (new edition), Longman, 1986.

Byrne, Donn, *Progressive Picture Compositions*, Longman, 1967.

Byrne, Donn, *Using the Magnetboard*, Heinemann Educational, 1980.

Byrne, Donn and Hall, Douglas, *Wall Pictures for Language Practice*, Longman, 1976.

Byrne, Donn and Wright, Andrew, *What Do You Think?*, Books 1 and 2, Longman, 1974.

Byrne, Donn and Wright, Andrew, *Say What You Think*, Longman, 1977.

Byrne, Donn and Rixon, Shelagh, *Communication Games* (ELT Guides Series), Nelson UK, Taylor and Francis, 1979.

Chuckney, William, *The Skeleton System*, copublished by Pilgrims Publications, Friendly Press and Hellenic, 1987.

Fletcher, M. and Birt, D., *Newsflash*, Edward Arnold, 1979.

Hadfield, Jill, *Elementary Communication Games*, Nelson, 1984.

Hadfield, Jill, *Advanced Communication Games*, Nelson, 1987.

Harkess, Shiona and Eastwood, John, *Cue for a Drill*, Oxford University Press, 1976.

Harkess, Shiona and Eastwood, John, *Cue for Communication*, Oxford University Press, 1980.

Heaton, J. B., *Composition Through Pictures*, Longman, 1966.

Holden, Susan (ed.), *Visual Aids for Classroom Interaction*, Modern English Publications, a subsidiary of Macmillan Publishers, 1978.

Jones, J. R. H., *Using the Overhead Projector*, Heinemann Educational, 1982.

Kerr, J. Y. K., *Picture Cue Cards for Oral Language Practice*, Evans Bros. and Bell Hyman, 1979.

McAlpin, Janet, *The Magazine Picture Library*, Heinemann Educational, 1980.

Maley, Alan and Duff, Alan, *Drama Techniques in Language Learning* (new edition), Cambridge University Press, 1982.

Maley, Alan, Duff, Alan and Grellet, Françoise, *The Mind's Eye*, Cambridge University Press, 1980.

Further reading

Morgan, John and Rinvolucri, Mario, *Once Upon a Time*, Cambridge University Press, 1983.

Mugglestone, Pat, *Planning and Using the Blackboard*, Heinemann Educational, 1981.

Scott, Wendy, *Are You Listening?*, Oxford University Press, 1980.

Shaw, Peter and de Vet, Therese, *Using Blackboard Drawing*, Heinemann Educational, 1980.

Spaventa, Lou (ed.), *Towards the Creative Teaching of English*, Heinemann Educational, 1987.

Wright, Andrew, *Visual Materials for the Language Teacher*, Longman, 1976.

Wright, Andrew, *1000 Pictures for Teachers to Copy*, Collins, 1984.

Wright, Andrew, Betteridge, David and Buckby, Michael, *Games for Language Learning* (new edition), Cambridge University Press, 1984.

Wright, Andrew, *How to Enjoy Paintings*, Cambridge University Press, 1986.

Wright, Andrew, *Visual Materials for the Language Teacher*, Longman, 1990.